INTERNATIONAL DEVELOPMENT IN FOCUS

# Unleashing E-Commerce for South Asian Integration

SANJAY KATHURIA, ARTI GROVER, VIVIANA MARIA EUGENIA PEREGO,
AADITYA MATTOO, AND PRITAM BANERJEE

**WORLD BANK GROUP**

# Contents

*Note:* The findings of this study are not binding on the countries covered by the study.

# Foreword

E-commerce helps integrate regions across the world and can be a powerful force for economic development. It can help make the international trading system more inclusive, for example, by allowing micro, small, and medium enterprises to access new markets and by letting consumers break through geographic barriers to reduce search and transaction costs.

In South Asia, e-commerce can play a much bigger role than it has thus far. While it has grown substantially in recent years, e-commerce in the region is still very small: even in India, online sales as a percentage of total retail sales were only 1.6 percent, versus over 15 percent for China and around 14 percent globally. Given that only a small share of firms has access to broadband connections and even fewer transact online, there is enormous room for e-commerce to grow in the region. For example, one forecast (Statista) shows that India, at a projected annual compound growth rate of almost 18 percent, will have the fastest growth of any country in retail e-commerce over 2019–23. Increasing use of e-commerce by consumers and firms in South Asia could potentially help increase competition and firm productivity, and encourage diversification of production and exports.

E-commerce and broader issues related to the digital economy can also lend themselves to controversy, such as that surrounding the enormous market power of large digital firms, or data localization. This report does not explore such topics.

Instead, it focuses on understanding key constraints to e-commerce in a region that is far behind other regions, including neighboring East Asia, with the aim of unleashing the positive power of e-commerce. Using a regional approach, the report addresses the regulatory complexities of e-commerce, and it explores issues such as data privacy, consumer protection, delivery, cybersecurity, market access regulations, and digital payments.

The report finds that ramping up e-commerce in the region would require significant coordination and cooperation between countries and between different government agencies and regulatory bodies. Knowing that the development of such coordination will be a slow-moving process, the report puts forward some interesting and innovative, yet practical, ideas that would help expand e-trade in South Asia. I can also sense the relevance of this approach to other regions in the world, particularly Africa and parts of Latin America and Eastern Europe.

I am confident that these ideas can help create a platform for a vigorous policy debate on a vital topic.

**Caroline Freund**
*Global Director*
*Trade, Investment, and Competitiveness*
*The World Bank*

# Acknowledgments

This report was prepared by a core team consisting of Sanjay Kathuria and Arti Grover (task leaders), Viviana Maria Eugenia Perego, Aaditya Mattoo, and Pritam Banerjee, and including Nadeem Rizwan and Ishita Dugar. Logistics support was provided by Grace James (Washington, D.C.), Savita Dhingra and Rima Sukhija (Delhi), Sashikala Krishani Jeyaraj (Colombo), and Priyanka Amatya (Kathmandu).

The work on the e-trade survey in South Asia was led by Martin Molinuevo (World Bank) and Kati Suominen (NexTrade). The team thanks the peer reviewers, Michael Joseph Ferrantino, Prasanna Lal Das, and Erik Nora, for their comments on the draft report. In addition, Michael Joseph Ferrantino generously shared his insights throughout the duration of the study. The work was done under the guidance of Manuela Francisco, Practice Manager, Macroeconomics, Trade, and Investment Global Practice, South Asia Region (and previously under Esperanza Lasagabaster, Practice Manager, Finance, Competitiveness, and Innovation Global Practice, South Asia Region), and under the overall direction of Robert J. Saum, then Director, Regional Integration, South Asia Region.

The team thanks the following colleagues and private sector counterparts for their help in coordinating consultation meetings: Pritam Banerjee (then with DHL, now Specialist Consultant at the Asian Development Bank), Priya Mathur, and the National Association of Software and Services Companies (NASSCOM; India); Ravindra Yatawara (Sri Lanka); and Ashish Narain and Rajan Krishna Panta (Nepal). These consultations have helped the team immensely, and included private sector firms and industry associations, as well as officials from relevant government agencies, in Sri Lanka, India, and Nepal.

The team thanks the Department for International Trade and Development for supporting this project as part of its overall support to the World Bank Group's regional integration program for South Asia. The work was also supported by the Umbrella Facility for Trade Trust Fund, a World Bank–administered multi-donor trust fund with contributions from the Department for International Development, Swedish International Development Cooperation Agency, State Secretariat for Economic Affairs, the Netherlands Ministry of Foreign Affairs, and the Norwegian Ministry of Foreign Affairs.

# About the Authors

**Pritam Banerjee** brings several years of experience in the areas of logistics operations, trade facilitation, and trade policy. He is currently a Consultant with the Asian Development Bank (ADB) as a Logistics Sector Specialist. Prior to his work with the ADB, Banerjee was Senior Director for Public Policy with the Deutsche Post DHL Group, responsible for South Asia. In this capacity, he was responsible for engaging with governments and governmental agencies on regulatory affairs and policy. He also served as a consultant for major clients of Deutsche Post DHL Group, finding solutions to regulatory and policy problems related to their supply chains. Banerjee previously served as the Head of Trade Policy, Confederation of Indian Industry's (CII) Trade Policy Division, and with the World Bank in Washington, D.C., where his work focused trade facilitation and trade in services. Banerjee is a member of the National Trade Facilitation Steering Committee and was most recently a special invitee to the Committee on Ease of Doing Business Reforms constituted under the Ministry of Commerce as a part of Prime Minister Modi's initiative on reforms. He serves as executive member of the Federation of Indian Chambers of Commerce and Industry (FICCI) Logistics Task Force, and he led FICCI's interaction on Goods and Services Tax (GST)–related issues relevant to the transport and logistics sector, focusing on operational aspects of GST implementation. He also serves as guest faculty at the Indian Institute of Foreign Trade (IIFT), Foreign Services Institute (FSI), and NACIN (National Academy of Customs, Indirect Taxes, and Narcotics). Banerjee has a PhD in public policy, and master's and undergraduate degrees in economics. He has been extensively published on issues related to international trade, regional integration, regulatory reforms, logistics and connectivity, and trade facilitation.

**Arti Grover** is a Senior Economist at the World Bank. She has extensive experience with complex analytical and operational projects on a range of topics including firm dynamics, trade, productivity, entrepreneurship, and spatial development. She has authored three books (on services trade, firm growth, and entrepreneurship), and her research has appeared in top peer-reviewed journals, as chapters in books, and as World Bank reports and policy research papers. Grover has been affiliated, in a research capacity, with the Harvard Business School and the Wharton School of the University of Pennsylvania. Prior to joining the Bank in 2009, Grover was a Doctoral Fulbright Fellow at Princeton University and an Assistant Professor at Delhi School of Economics, India.

**Sanjay Kathuria** is Lead Economist and Coordinator, South Asia Regional Integration, in the World Bank's Macroeconomics, Trade, and Investment Global Practice, based in Washington, DC. During his more than 27 years at the World Bank, he has worked in several regions, including Europe and Central Asia, Latin America and the Caribbean, and South Asia. Prior to joining the World Bank, he was a Fellow at the Indian Council for Research on International Economic Relations in New Delhi. He graduated from St. Stephen's College, and he received his master's degree from the Delhi School of Economics and his doctorate from Oxford University. His research interests include economic growth, international trade and trade policy, economic integration, competitiveness, technology development, fiscal policy, and financial sector development.

**Aaditya Mattoo** is Chief Economist of the East Asia and Pacific Region of the World Bank. He specializes in development, trade, and international cooperation, and provides policy advice to governments. He is also Co-Director of the *World Development Report 2020* on global value chains. Prior to this, he was the Research Manager, Trade and Integration, at the World Bank. Before joining the Bank, he was Economic Counselor at the World Trade Organization and taught economics at the University of Sussex and Churchill College, Cambridge University. He holds a PhD in economics from the University of Cambridge, and an MPhil in economics from the University of Oxford. He has published on development, trade, trade in services, and international trade agreements in academic and other journals, and his work has been cited in the *Economist*, *Financial Times*, *New York Times*, and *Time* magazine.

**Viviana Maria Eugenia Perego** is an Economist at the World Bank, where she works on themes related to competitiveness, agriculture, and rural livelihoods. Her current projects focus on productive alliances in agriculture, the efficiency of special economic zones, disruptive technologies, the labor market integration of fragile populations, and food systems' resilience to climate change. Viviana holds a DPhil (PhD) in economics from the University of Oxford, from which she graduated in 2017 with a thesis on the drivers of development in open economies. Prior to joining the World Bank, she collaborated with institutions such as the International Labour Organization, UNICEF, and the Bank of Italy, as well as leading research centers such as J-PAL (Abdul Latif Jameel Poverty Action Lab) at the Massachusetts Institute of Technology and the Centre for the Study of African Economies at Oxford.

# Abbreviations

| | |
|---|---|
| BBIN | Bangladesh, Bhutan, India, and Nepal (subregion) |
| B2B | business-to-business e-commerce |
| B2C | business-to-consumer e-commerce |
| B2G | business-to-government e-commerce |
| CPTPP | Comprehensive and Progressive Agreement for Trans-Pacific Partnership |
| e-ID | electronic identification program |
| EU | European Union |
| FDI | foreign direct investment |
| GDP | gross domestic product |
| ICT | information and communications technology |
| IP | Internet protocol |
| ISP | Internet service provider |
| IT | information technology |
| MVA | motor vehicle agreement |
| OECD | Organisation for Economic Co-operation and Development |
| PISP | payment initiation service provider |
| PSP | payment system provider |
| SMEs | small and medium enterprises |
| UNCTAD | United Nations Conference on Trade and Development |
| USITC | U.S. International Trade Commission |
| USTR | Office of the U.S. Trade Representative |

# Introduction

E-commerce is dramatically changing the way goods and services are transacted regionally, nationally, and globally. The Internet seamlessly connects buyers and sellers otherwise separated by geographical distances and logistical barriers and makes transactions convenient, fast, and efficient. In 2017, a total of US$2.3 trillion was spent globally by retail consumers, almost 25 percent more than in 2016. This figure is expected to grow to more than US$4 trillion by 2020, reaching more than 15 percent of total retail spending, from around 10 percent in 2015.[1] E-commerce facilitates international trade by reducing the cost of distance and remoteness. For example, the presence of a digital platform could substantially reduce the costs of connecting buyers and suppliers with markets. A few empirical papers have also formally established the link between Internet and digital commerce, on the one side, and consumer welfare and other measures of economic benefits, on the other. These studies suggest that e-commerce and online business activity stimulate nonnegligible consumer gains,[2] entrepreneurship,[3] job growth,[4] international trade,[5] gross domestic product (GDP), revenues, and productivity.[6] As such, its development potential may be realized along several channels, including enhanced participation in international value chains, increased market access and reach, and improved internal and market efficiency, as well as lower transaction costs.[7]

E-commerce can potentially be more inclusive of underrepresented groups such as women, small businesses, and rural entrepreneurs. The benefits of e-commerce are well reflected in the case of China, where, for instance, Alibaba alone is reported to have created 30 million job opportunities, most notably among young people, rural communities, and disadvantaged groups (Wei 2017). E-commerce can enable small companies to transcend geographic boundaries and gain higher international visibility; or provide opportunities for more flexible employment to otherwise marginalized socioeconomic groups, such as women; or otherwise benefit those living in remote areas, countering the forces of agglomeration effects (Goldfarb and Tucker 2017).

South Asia lags the rest of the world in activating the potential benefits from e-commerce. There is a large disparity in the extent of online purchases across the world. In 2015, online sales as a percentage of total retail sales were more than 15 percent in China and in the United Kingdom, and more than 11 percent in the Republic of Korea, but were 1.6 percent in India (data from eMarketer) and around 0.7 percent in Bangladesh (Bansal 2017).

There are also wide variations within South Asia. Of those firms in South Asia that are connected to the Internet, about 50 percent of them market and sell online, and fewer than 40 percent purchase online (figure I.1). Moreover, intraregional variation in information and communications technology (ICT) uptake is substantial. Figure I.1 illustrates that while Indians and Pakistanis make significant use of online connectivity, other countries, such as Bangladesh and Nepal, fare worse than many African countries along most e-commerce indicators.

Recent evidence from a World Bank report (Kathuria 2018) points to the low levels of intraregional trade on the subcontinent. Although intraregional trade accounts for 50 percent of regional total trade in East Asia and Pacific and 22 percent in Sub-Saharan Africa, in South Asia, the figure amounts to only 5 percent. Evidence indicates that current trade in goods within South Asia is one-third of its potential, and trade among Bangladesh, India, and Pakistan in particular has been estimated to be well below its potential. This shortfall stems from high tariffs and para-tariffs, disproportionately high trade costs due to poor logistical infrastructure and inefficient trade facilitation, the existence of complicated and nontransparent nontariff measures, constraints on services trade, below-potential foreign direct investment (FDI), and the lack of regional value chains. In addition, the pervasive lack of mutual trust between countries in the region hurts trade. Such barriers negate the benefit of geographical and cultural proximity.

**FIGURE I.1**

**E-commerce activities of South Asian firms**

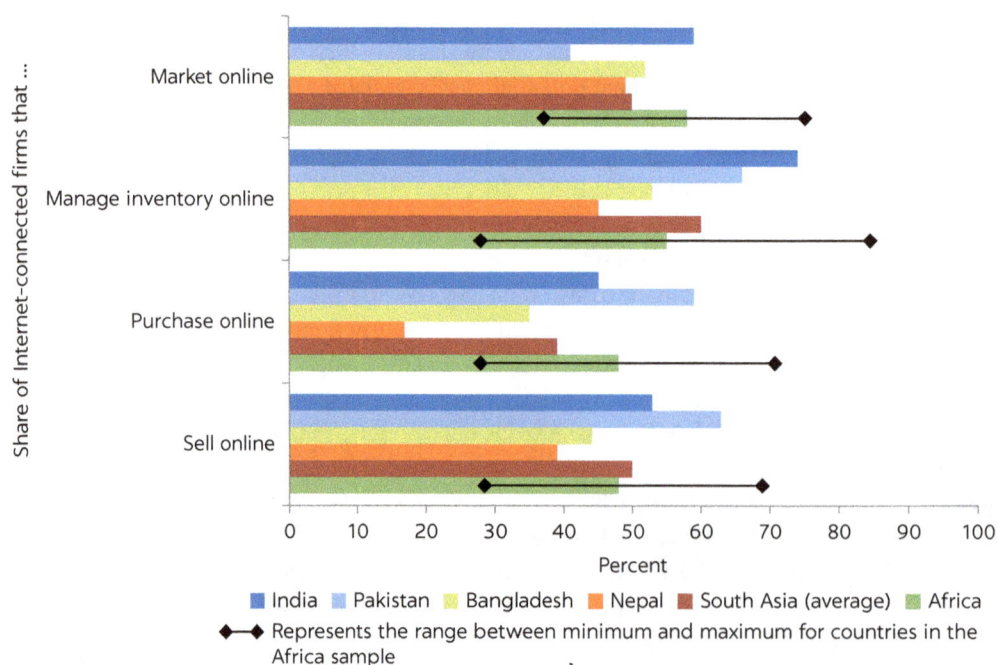

*Source:* Lopez-Acevedo, Medvedev, and Palmade 2017.

An e-commerce survey reaffirmed the lack of intraregional trade in South Asia. As part of this study, a survey of more than 2,200 firms showed that most of their cross-border e-commerce was conducted with extraregional partners, such as China, the United Kingdom, and the United States.

Given the potential of e-commerce to connect distant markets, it is possible that e-commerce can also strengthen commercial linkages within South Asia and bring gains to consumers and small players. Through Internet communication, e-commerce has the potential to stimulate regional trade by bridging the gap between buyers and sellers on different sides of national borders. Evidence indicates that the Internet increases trade in physical goods (Borga and Koncz-Bruner 2011; Freund and Weinhold 2004; Olarreaga and Sidley Austin 2012) and digital services (Alaveras and Martens 2015; Blum and Goldfarb 2006; Lendle et al. 2016). According to the e-commerce survey previously cited, if the top three hurdles to e-commerce in the region were resolved, there would be significant gains in exports and employment. Although the gains would be similar across firms of all sizes, they would tend to be higher in countries with a larger share of online sellers (see chapter 2 for more details). Apart from firms, consumers in South Asia stand to gain significantly from the potential reduction in costs and availability of a greater variety of e-traded goods and services.

This report presents a conceptual framework for understanding the regulatory constraints on e-commerce through the private sector's perspective. Using this framework, the report seeks specifically to illuminate (a) the role that e-commerce can play in reducing transaction costs, (b) the regulations that complement or hinder e-commerce in reducing these costs, and (c) how firms engaged in the e-commerce space adjust to suboptimal modes of operation. Using this framework and consultations with private sector participants in India (Delhi and Bangalore), Nepal (Kathmandu), and Sri Lanka (Colombo), the report proposes to disentangle the complex mechanisms that prevent cross-border e-commerce from thriving in the region, as identified by key private sector players.[8] In addition to these consultations, the report also analyzes the results of the E-Commerce Development Survey, which was designed by the World Bank and Nextrade Group. Finally, the report uses this framework to propose an initial set of ideas that could increase e-commerce within South Asia.

Despite the incipient nature of e-commerce in most countries in the region, there is growing evidence of the possibilities for cross-border e-commerce. For example, there is some degree of informal e-trade across the land borders, and there are other high-demand goods and services that could easily be mediated by e-commerce. Moreover, with 28 percent of the region's population younger than age 15, the millions of young people who can become consumers, entrepreneurs, and technicians can expand South Asia's e-commerce potential significantly.

The report suggests a practical approach toward developing cross-border e-commerce in South Asia, building on formal and informal cross-border trade. The suggestions focus on the simplification of tariff, payment, and logistical barriers to e-commerce, which were found to be the most immediate constraints on e-commerce firms operating across borders. To begin, consumers would ride on the reputation of big e-commerce firms as a substitute for formal, robust contractual and consumer protection mechanisms.

The report is organized as follows: Chapter 1 begins by describing e-commerce and then presents a conceptual framework for how e-commerce can reduce transaction costs. It also presents the modes of operation for firms engaging in digital space. Chapter 2 summarizes the results of the E-Commerce

Development Survey. Chapter 3 presents an overview of the state of regulations prevailing in South Asia and the specific enabling reforms that are needed at the national and international levels for e-commerce to flourish in the region. Chapter 4 proposes concrete policy implications for the construction of a unified digital South Asian market. Chapter 5 provides a menu of policy options. Chapter 6 concludes and offers practical options to kick-start the formal e-commerce market in South Asia.

The report mostly focuses on business-to-consumer (B2C) e-commerce and cross-border issues. Hence, it does not deal with other interesting categories of e-commerce, such as business-to-business (B2B) and business-to-government (B2G). The report is not a substitute for country-specific e-commerce studies, although country policies do need to be referenced in different chapters of the report because regional e-trade builds on the framework set by national e-commerce policies. And although many of the recommendations would apply to goods and services, specific constraints on e-trade in services are not a focus area of the report.

Future areas of analysis on e-commerce in South Asia should include services and informal trade. The possibilities for regional e-trade in services are high, such as in health, education, and professional services. Such trade can be intermediated via e-commerce and hence made more efficient, such as in improved search for doctors and delivery of first-stage doctor consultation services via the Internet. E-commerce can also help catalyze improvements in the regulatory environment for specific services, as is suggested in this report in the case of e-transport in South Asia. Another area for future analysis could involve more in-depth coverage of informal e-trade, including field studies of those who are involved in such trade.

This report is part of a larger work program on building a more positive narrative on regional integration in South Asia. It is a follow-up to the recent flagship report, *A Glass Half Full: The Promise of Regional Trade in South Asia* (Kathuria 2018), produced as part of that program. By focusing on knowledge generation, convening and capacity building, and communications, the program seeks to help gradually shape a more positive narrative. Other elements of a broader work program on regional integration in South Asia include connectivity, water, and climate change, with details available on the World Bank website, https://www.worldbank.org/en/programs/south-asia-regional-integration.

## NOTES

1. From Statista (https://www.statista.com/statistics/379046/worldwide-retail-e-commerce-sales).
2. For example, Brynjolfsson, Hu, and Smith (2003) focus on the consumer surplus generated by the increased product variety available at online booksellers in the United States. Fan et al. (2016) document an increase in access to consumption varieties and a reduction in income inequality among smaller and remote Chinese cities, which they attribute to the reduction in transaction costs through e-commerce. Likewise, using U.S. data on the travel agency, bookstore, and new car dealer industries, Goldmanis et al. (2010) show that e-commerce reallocates market shares from high-cost to low-cost producers and reduces search costs for consumers buying from heterogeneous firms. Related to these studies, Goolsbee and Klenow (2006) estimate changes in equivalent variation (a measure of consumer welfare) from residential Internet usage in the United States.
3. Huang et al. (2018) measure the variations of e-commerce development across counties in China and assess its impact on entrepreneurship in rural and urban areas. Their study

suggests that households living in counties with higher levels of e-commerce development are more likely to run their own businesses and experience significant increases in the entry of new startups as well as decreases in the exit of incumbent businesses.

4. In particular, Hjort and Poulsen (2016) study the effect of fast-speed Internet on labor markets in 14 African countries and find a positive effect on overall employment, driven by an expansion of higher-skill employment. Other studies in this field include Deighton, Kornfeld, and Gerra (2012) and McKinsey Global Institute (2011).

5. See, for example, Borga and Koncz-Bruner (2011) and Olarreaga and Sidley Austin (2012).

6. See Bughin et al. (2011), Dean et al. (2012), Goyal (2010), McKinsey Global Institute (2011), and Olarreaga and Sidley Austin (2012).

7. Using a rich dataset on prices, quantities, and characteristics of three consumer electronics products in several European countries in 2008–09, a study finds that consumers capture on average 83 percent of the total welfare gains induced by e-commerce (relative to firms). These benefits arise largely from increased product differentiation (Duch-Brown, Grzybowski, and Verboven 2015). As for firms, online activity also raises their labor productivity. For example, an analysis of e-sales of firms in 14 European Union countries suggests that an increase in electronic sales raises the rate of labor productivity by 0.3 percentage point over a two-year window in the sample period 2002–10 (Falk and Hagsten 2015).

8. In addition to the private sector firms, semistructured interviews were also conducted with reputed law firms, the Central Bank of Nepal, think tanks, and industry associations.

## REFERENCES

Alaveras, Georgios, and Bertin Martens. 2015. "International Trade in Online Services." Digital Economy Working Paper No. 2015-08. Institute of Prospective Technological Studies, European Commission, Brussels.

Bansal, Varsha. 2017. "Global Investors Heading to India Are Beginning to Make a Stopover at Bangladesh." *Economic Times*, November 17. https://economictimes.indiatimes.com/small -biz/startups/features/global-investors-heading-to-india-are-beginning-to-make-a -stopover-at-bangladesh/articleshow/61678920.cms?from=mdr.

Blum, Bernardo S., and Avi Goldfarb. 2006. "Does the Internet Defy the Law of Gravity?" *Journal of International Economics* 70 (2): 384–405.

Borga, Maria, and Jennifer Koncz-Bruner. 2011. *Trends in Digitally-Enabled Trade in Services.* Washington, DC: U.S. Department of Commerce, Bureau of Economic Analysis.

Brynjolfsson, Erik, Yu Hu, and Michael. D. Smith. 2003. "Consumer Surplus in the Digital Economy: Estimating the Value of Increased Product Variety at Online Booksellers." *Management Science* 49 (11): 1580–96.

Bughin, Jacques, Laura Corb, James Manyika, Olivia Nottebohm, Michael Chui, Borja de Muller Barbat, and Remi Said. 2011. *The Impact of Internet Technologies: Search.* McKinsey & Company, High Tech Practice.

Dean, David, Sebastian Digrande, Dominic Field, Andreas Lundmark, James O'Day, John Pineda, and Paul Zwillenberg. 2012. *The $4.2 Trillion Opportunity: The Internet Economy in the G-20.* Connected World Series. Boston: Boston Consulting Group.

Deighton, John, Leora Kornfeld, and M. Gerra. 2012. *Economic Value of the Advertising-Supported Internet Ecosystem.* New York: Interactive Advertising Bureau.

Duch-Brown, Néstor, Lukasz Grzybowski, and Frank Verboven. 2015. "The Impact of Online Sales on Consumers and Firms: Evidence from Household Appliances." Working Paper 2015-15, Institute for Prospective Technological Studies Digital Economy European Commission.

Falk, Martin, and Eva Hagsten. 2015. "E-Commerce Trends and Impacts across Europe." *International Journal of Production Economics* 170: 357–69.

Fan, Jingting, Lixin Tang, Weiming Zhu, and Ben Zou. 2016. "The Alibaba Effect: Spatial Consumption Inequality and the Welfare Gains from E-Commerce." Unpublished paper, Michigan State University, East Lansing.

Freund, Caroline, and Diana Weinhold. 2004. "The Effect of the Internet on International Trade." *Journal of International Economics* 62 (1): 171–89.

Goldfarb, Avi, and Catherine Tucker. 2017. "Digital Economics." NBER Working Paper No. 23684, National Bureau of Economic Research, Cambridge, MA.

Goldmanis, Maris, Ali Hortaçsu, Chad Syverson, and Önsel Emre. 2010. "E-Commerce and the Market Structure of Retail Industries." *Economic Journal* 120 (545): 651–82.

Goolsbee, Austan, and Peter J. Klenow. 2006. "Valuing Consumer Products by the Time Spent Using Them: An Application to the Internet." *American Economic Review* 96 (2): 108–13.

Goyal, Aparajita. 2010. "Information, Direct Access to Farmers, and Rural Market Performance in Central India." *American Economic Journal: Applied Economics* 2 (3): 22–45.

Hjort, Jonas, and Jonas Poulsen. 2016. "The Arrival of Fast Internet and Skilled Job Creation in Africa." Unpublished paper, Columbia University, New York.

Huang, Bihong, Mohamed Shaban, Quanyun Song, and Yu Wu. 2018. "E-Commerce Development and Entrepreneurship in the People's Republic of China." Working Paper 827, Asian Development Bank, Mandaluyong, Philippines. https://www.adb.org /publications/e-commerce-development-and-entrepreneurship-prc.

Kathuria, Sanjay. 2018. *A Glass Half Full: The Promise of Regional Trade in South Asia.* Washington, DC: World Bank.

Lendle, Andreas, Marcelo Olarreaga, Simon Schropp, and Pierre-Louis Vézina. 2016. "There Goes Gravity: eBay and the Death of Distance." *Economic Journal* 126 (591): 406–41.

Lopez-Acevedo, Gladys, Denis Medvedev, and Vincent Palmade. 2017. *South Asia's Turn: Policies to Boost Competitiveness and Create the Next Export Powerhouse.* Conference Edition. Washington, DC: World Bank.

McKinsey Global Institute. 2011. *Internet Matters: The Net's Sweeping Impact on Growth, Jobs, and Prosperity.* New York: McKinsey Global Institute.

Olarreaga, M., and Sidley Austin LLP. 2012. *Enabling Traders to Enter and Grow on the Global Stage: The Story of an Online Marketplace.* Washington, DC: eBay.

Wei, He. 2017. "Alibaba Creates 30 Million Jobs." *China Daily*, January 4. http://www.chinadaily .com.cn/business/2017-01/04/content_27853067.htm.

# 1 Understanding E-Commerce

## WHAT IS E-COMMERCE?

*E-commerce* can be defined as doing business over the Internet, selling goods and services that can be transacted online and then delivered offline or digitized and delivered online, such as computer software (Coppel 2000). The most common transactions on digital markets can be broadly classified into online travel (for example, airline tickets and other transport and hotel booking) and nontravel. Nontravel, in turn, features online retail (e-tailing), utilities, and other services. The e-tailing segment spans a broad commodity range, from food, to vehicles, to lifestyle products (see table 1.1 for a global picture), but certain products tend to be more "digitally tradable" than others. In India, for example, the most highly traded products fall under the categories of mobile phones, electronic and computer accessories, clothing, footwear, fashion accessories, and consumer durables (IAMAI and Kantar IMRB 2016). As for cross-border e-tail transactions, eBay reports that in India the most highly traded products on its platform are jewelry, health and beauty products, clothing and accessories, and home furnishings. For example, in India, a fast-selling product such as jewelry is exported every 5 seconds, while toys or a musical instrument are exported only every 12–15 minutes (FICCI CMSME 2017).

### How does e-commerce reduce transaction costs?

The benefits of e-commerce are realized through a reduction in transaction costs. With the advent of the digital economy, it is easier to find and compare information about products and services from different providers, which drives down search costs (Goldfarb and Tucker 2017). The use of standardized, automatic online processes and secure payment gateways, in turn, reduces contracting and payment costs. Finally, e-commerce has strongly redefined the concept of distance and remoteness, eventually decreasing transport and delivery costs for consumers. The introduction of e-commerce into an industry can be associated with a decline in equilibrium of average price levels and dispersion, together with a shift in market share toward more productive firms (Goldmanis et al. 2010). Another indicator of lower transaction costs is the facilitation of matching

**TABLE 1.1 Product sales by major e-commerce players**

| AMAZON | EBAY | ALIBABA |
|--------|------|---------|
| Computers and computer accessories | Audio and home entertainment | Agriculture |
| Sports, fitness, and outdoors | Automotive | Food and beverages |
| Handbags and luggage | Baby and mom | Apparel |
| Cameras, audio, and video | Beauty, health, and grocery | Textile and leather products |
| Beauty, health, and groceries | Books and magazines | Fashion accessories |
| Books | Cameras and optics | Timepieces, jewelry, and eyewear |
| Shoes | Charity | Automobiles and motorcycles |
| Clothing and accessories | Clothing and accessories | Transportation |
| Movies, music, and video games | Coins and notes | Luggage, bags, and cases |
| Home, kitchen, and pets | Collectibles | Shoes and accessories |
| Jewelry, watches, and eyewear | eBay daily | Computer hardware and software |
| Cars, motorbikes, and industrial | Games, consoles, and accessories | Home appliances |
| Mobiles and tablets | Home and kitchen appliances | Consumer electronics |
| Toys and baby products | Home and living | Security and protection |
| Used and refurbished phones, electronics, etc. | Jewelry and precious coins | Electrical equipment and supplies |
| | Kitchen and dining | Telecommunication |
| | Laptops and computer peripherals | Sports and entertainment |
| | LCD, LED, and televisions | Gifts and crafts |
| | Memory cards, pen drives, and HDD | Toys and hobbies |
| | Mobile accessories | Health and medical |
| | Movies and music | Beauty and personal care |
| | Musical instruments | Construction and real estate |
| | Shoes | Home and garden |
| | Sports, fitness, and outdoors | Lights and lighting |
| | Stamps | Furniture |
| | Stationery and office supplies | Machinery |
| | Tablets and accessories | Industrial parts and fabrication services |
| | Tools, hardware, and electricals | Tools |
| | Toys, games, and school supplies | Hardware |

*Source:* FICCI CMSME 2017.

through online trade, which serves as an intermediary between buyers and sellers (Jullien 2012; Nocke, Peitz, and Stahl 2007) and increases the efficiency of trade itself, as it enables providers to cater to a large number of customers, leveraging the interoperability of Internet services (Hagiu 2012).

Furthermore, e-commerce may provide innovative ways to address policy-induced transaction costs. For example, it may enhance cross-border sales if its diffusion facilitates the setting up of an appropriate tariff program for low-value imports, de facto circumventing the market distortions induced by taxation and duties. At the same time, the development of e-commerce might result in a more efficient achievement of various regulatory objectives and, consequently, reduce the costs of complying with the regulation itself. For instance, customer feedback mechanisms and the fear of reputational damage generally push e-commerce firms to establish various forms of self-regulation in the field of consumer protection, which are usually significantly more consumer-friendly than the national law itself. The first two columns in figure 1.1 summarize this conceptual framework, distinguishing between policy and nonpolicy transaction costs and highlighting the direct or indirect effect of e-commerce on each. The last column in the figure identifies the main barriers that can hinder the diffusion of e-commerce, affecting its potential as a source of inclusive growth.

Structural gaps in the socioeconomic and business environments explain much of the lag in e-commerce adoption by developing countries. The lack of basic infrastructure, such as all-season roads or efficient transportation and logistics infrastructure, poses significant constraints on internal trade in poorer countries. Poor quality of basic information and communications technology (ICT) infrastructure and low computer penetration further inhibit the diffusion of e-commerce. In addition, low levels of digital literacy and awareness are a cause for concern in developing countries. Most micro and small enterprises in low- and middle-income countries lack information on the possibilities afforded by digital technologies—and even if this were not the case, the workforce is usually not educated in basic ICT skills or more sophisticated organizational skills, such as order handling, quality control, and processing of online payments.

Alongside such logistical constraints, there are regulatory and institutional barriers to e-commerce. As listed in figure 1.1, restrictive policies or the lack of enabling reforms in the areas of data privacy, consumer protection, cybersecurity, e-transactions, and e-signatures, together with competition rules that do not account for the specificities of the digital economy, can be as detrimental to e-commerce diffusion as the structural gaps. Empirical research

**FIGURE 1.1**

**Conceptual framework**

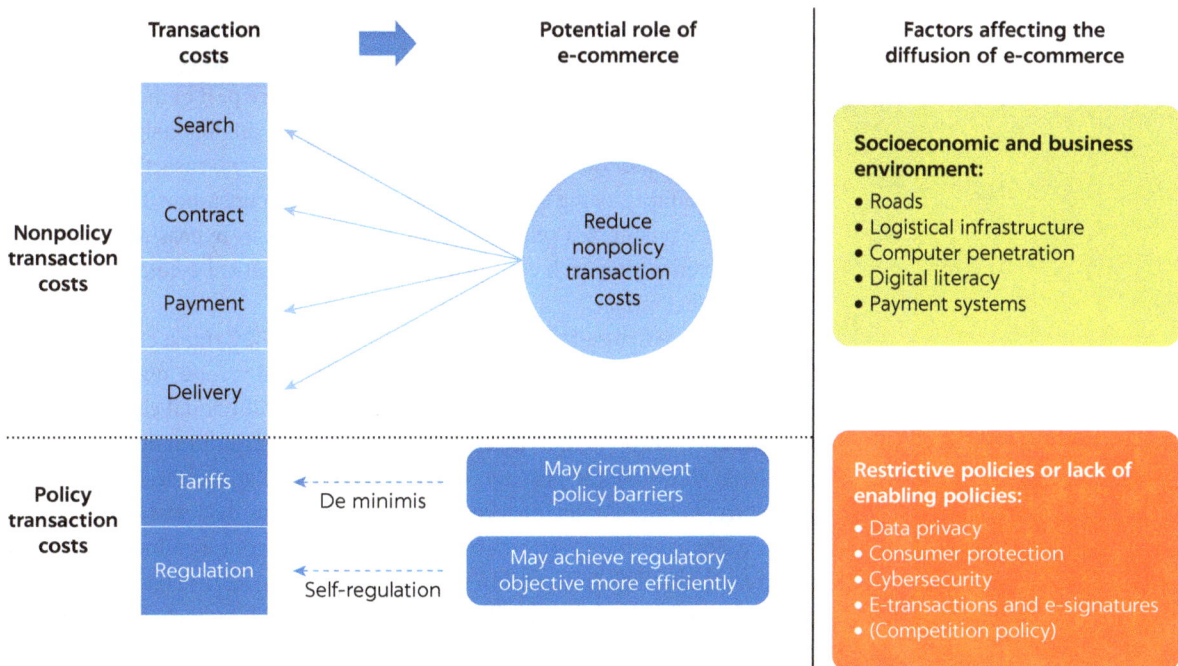

*Source:* Original analysis.

has established that regulatory and legal e-commerce barriers are key in explaining the slow diffusion of e-commerce in many parts of the world.[1] Moreover, an improved regulatory framework can be designed relatively easily in the short run, whereas infrastructural upgrade is likely to require costly investment and takes a longer time to complete. This report focuses on the regulatory barriers to e-commerce that can be easily rectified, for South Asian countries to start building a conducive framework for e-commerce in a reasonably short time frame, exploiting the existing logistical infrastructure. Regulatory and legal barriers are among the main obstacles that slow the pace of e-commerce diffusion in the developing world (Kshetri 2007). The E-Commerce Development Survey, conducted as part of this project, shows that regulatory constraints on e-commerce and digital payments particularly hurt small firms.[2] Evidence from a phone survey of high-ranking managers from more than 2,100 business establishments in 10 countries[3] identified regulatory issues in the field of privacy, data security, and the legal status of e-transactions as the biggest barriers to e-commerce adoption.[4] Data from the same survey show that small firms in South Asia view customs procedures for e-commerce shipment as one of the major challenges for developing e-commerce in the region. Likewise, digital payments are a big constraint, especially in the context of cross-border transactions. Surveyed small and medium-size enterprises (SMEs) reported that removing regulatory and logistical challenges to e-commerce would increase their exports, employment, and productivity by as much as 20–30 percent. Meetings with the private sector conducted by the World Bank team in Nepal, India, and Sri Lanka corroborated these challenges and highlighted other regulatory constraints pertaining to consumer protection.

## What are the operating models for firms in digital space?

Various models of digital trade exist, each involving a different combination of parties (OECD 2017). For instance, business-to-government (B2G) transactions see businesses selling to governments; business-to-business (B2B) transactions involve two enterprises (including when enterprises are part of the same group, as is the case for multinational corporations); and, analogously, consumer-to-consumer transactions involve two consumers directly transacting with each other (for example, using eBay). Finally, business-to-consumer (B2C) transactions involve businesses selling directly to households, bypassing traditional retailers. Even within each category, the variety of practical e-commerce applications is substantial.

E-commerce firms—for example, those engaged in B2C transactions in goods or services—operate with a range of business models. First, one must distinguish between single-brand, stand-alone websites, where individual companies sell their products through their own electronic portal, and multibrand, online platforms that showcase the products of multiple sellers. Each of these major models, in turn, is an umbrella for several different solutions that can be observed in practice. For example, firms such as Amazon and Flipkart are online portals with multibrand retailing. Even within these broader platforms, the big e-commerce players have three sets of possible models: inventory-based, marketplace, and online malls. Other possibilities involve a combination of these three models. The identified models, with some examples of South Asian firms in each category, are visualized in figure 1.2.

**FIGURE 1.2**

**Operating models of firms in the e-commerce space**

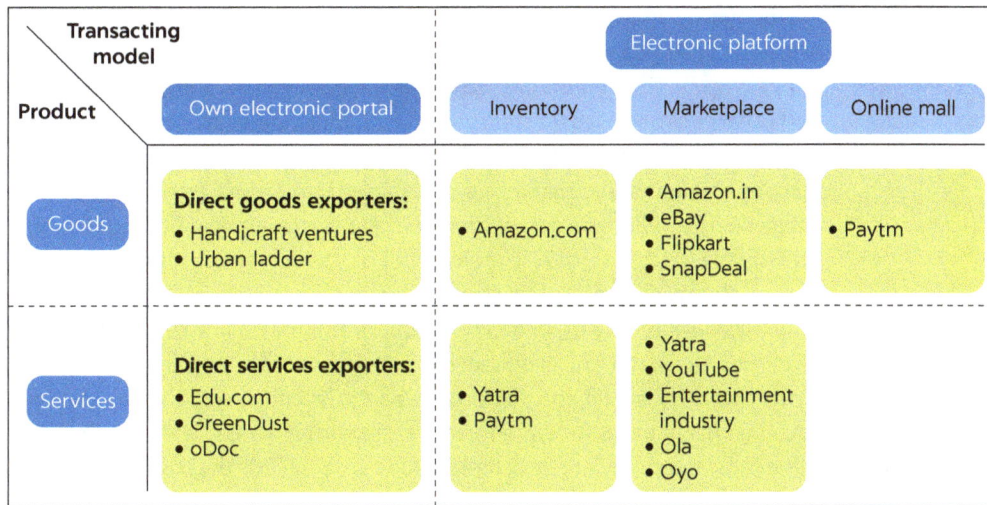

| Transacting model / Product | Own electronic portal | Electronic platform | | |
|---|---|---|---|---|
| | | Inventory | Marketplace | Online mall |
| **Goods** | **Direct goods exporters:**<br>• Handicraft ventures<br>• Urban ladder | • Amazon.com | • Amazon.in<br>• eBay<br>• Flipkart<br>• SnapDeal | • Paytm |
| **Services** | **Direct services exporters:**<br>• Edu.com<br>• GreenDust<br>• oDoc | • Yatra<br>• Paytm | • Yatra<br>• YouTube<br>• Entertainment industry<br>• Ola<br>• Oyo | |

*Source:* Original analysis.

In the stand-alone model, an e-commerce firm sells its products through its own website. This can be established in various ways, from adding an e-commerce function to an existing website; to using a "software as a service" solution (using website templates that have all the features needed for e-commerce); to building an ad hoc, customized e-commerce site. These options span different levels of flexibility and demand in terms of resources and technical skills. On the one hand, low-cost solutions are relatively straightforward to set up and operate but might result in unprofessional-looking websites and less-than-efficient services. On the other hand, more customized solutions are better tailored to the firm's needs but are more expensive and more demanding in ICT-intensive skills. In India, Handicraft Ventures and GreenDust are examples of firms that provide niche goods and services, respectively, and that have been able to set up their own electronic portals. Handicraft Ventures is engaged in manufacturing and exporting customized, handmade Indian artifacts and products to Europe and the United States. The products offered by the firm range from brass designer handicrafts, to leather products, to sculptures and paintings, with an emphasis on the premium quality and uniqueness of each piece. GreenDust is a reverse logistics firm and online shopping site. After collecting unused, branded factory seconds, surplus, overstock, and refurbished products (mostly electronics) from manufacturers and repairing them, the firm offers customers and bulk buyers the option to purchase these products at discount prices on its platform. In Sri Lanka, oDoc provides consumers with access to electronic consultations with doctors,

Electronic or online platforms are third-party marketplaces for marketing and selling products online. They may differ in the geographical focus (purely national, or open to international buyers or sellers, or both) and in the range of services offered (like showcasing, payment solutions, and handling of orders). Regardless of the geographical scope, three different models for online platforms can be identified: (a) pure marketplace, (b) online mall, and (c) self-owned inventory. In the pure marketplace model, sellers offer their products on the marketplace's website, where the products are showcased along with those of competitors. The *marketplace* may offer additional services—like advertising, customer relations, and delivery—but sellers need to manage their inventory autonomously. eBay is an example of the marketplace model. Among service firms, the most prominent marketplaces for tradable services are in the travel business (examples in India are yatra.com and makemytrip.com), whereas localized services can be used for transport (for example, Ola is the Indian equivalent of Uber or Lyft) or for apartment renting (in India and many other countries, Oyo functions as a hotel chain as well and has moved into Airbnb-type homestays). In *online malls*, a seller partners with a marketplace to set up a dedicated online store on the latter's website. The store will be a single-brand entity, where customers can browse the entire range of products sold online by the company rather than searching by item. Here, sellers still play a key role in managing inventory. An example of an online mall is Paytm in India. In the case of the *self-owned inventory* model, the platform owns the inventory and controls delivery, and thus has more efficient control of the supply chain, warehousing, and shipments. Amazon, Snapdeal, and Alibaba are probably the best-known international examples of this model, although regulatory barriers on foreign ownership prevent them from holding their own inventories in many South Asian countries (see the next section). The model allows for smoother operations and overall better customer relations (quality control and handling of complaints, returns, and refunds) and shifts the burden of inventory risk to the platform.

### How do regulations distort the operating models of e-commerce firms?

Each model has its own advantages, which determine a firm's choice on the basis of its characteristics. For example, consultations with private sector players—such as Handicraft Ventures in India, Takas in Sri Lanka, and Muncha in Nepal—suggest that own portals are the preferred transacting model for firms that are relatively well established. Own electronic portals could also be more suitable when the firm sells nonstandardized and niche products. A stand-alone website offers more flexibility in functionalities, payment options, geographical scope, and design, and it does not have to conform to third-party policies (for example, on returns and refunds or stringent and expensive inventory requirements). As a result, firms with a strong brand or relatively higher capabilities, or those selling niche products, may find it optimal to work through their own portals. Selling on platforms, by contrast, allows the seller to leverage the platform's reputation, infrastructure, and existing pool of buyers, which makes platforms particularly suitable for smaller firms or companies offering standardized products. Smaller sellers are likely to benefit the most from inventory-type platforms, which allow them to operate online even with limited logistical capabilities.

Firm choice is distorted by existing regulations in South Asia. For example, in countries such as India and Sri Lanka, foreign multibrand retailers cannot have their own inventory, and international giants like Amazon, Flipkart, and Daraz must operate as pure marketplaces. This may have consequences for market access for small firms with limited digital and logistical skills because it reduces the options available to these small retailers and producers (for example, in their ability to hold inventory and manage liquidity).

Restrictions on payment methods and foreign exchange controls can have a substantial impact on the strategic choices of private sector players, especially when dealing with cross-border transactions. Field interviews in Sri Lanka and Nepal revealed how some entrepreneurs, to sell more conveniently in international marketplaces, open subsidiaries overseas (for example, in Australia, Singapore, or the United States). Although this allows them to receive international payments and fulfill international orders, it may not be the most efficient method of operation because it involves additional overhead and transaction costs.

## NOTES

1. Bastos Tigre and Dedrick (2004) report inadequate regulation on privacy and security, lack of business laws for e-commerce, inadequate legal protection for Internet purchases, and concern about Internet taxation as the key issues identified by Brazilian consumers on low e-commerce adoption. In China, the lack of transactional and institutional trust related to the weak rule of law represents a major impediment to e-commerce (Efendioglu and Yip 2004; Gibbs, Kraemer, and Dedrick 2003). Similarly, Oxley and Yeung (2001) show that e-commerce activity depends on a supportive institutional environment, and Shih, Dedrick, and Kraemer (2005) find that the rule of law is an important factor determining the willingness of businesses and consumers to engage in e-commerce. Moreover, Shih, Dedrick, and Kraemer show that various potential facilitators or enablers of e-commerce (like financial resources, experience with direct marketing, and availability of payment facilitators) only matter when the rule of law is strong. They report that firms worldwide identify regulatory issues in the field of privacy, data security, and e-transactions as the biggest barriers to e-commerce adoption. More recently, Couture et al. (2017) find that, when not accompanied by other complementary interventions to support the transition to local online trading activity, the benefits of e-commerce are unlikely to materialize in the short to medium run.
2. This survey covers 1,688 merchants in seven economies (Afghanistan, Bangladesh, Bhutan, India, Nepal, Pakistan, and Sri Lanka), across nine major sectors, and 539 e-commerce ecosystem firms (such as e-commerce and payment platforms and logistics, financial services, and IT services firms).
3. The economies are Brazil; China; Denmark; France; Germany; Japan; Mexico; Singapore; Taiwan, China; and the United States.
4. See Shih, Dedrick, and Kraemer (2005). Nonetheless, regulatory changes need to be complemented by better institutions, such as the rule of law (Oxley and Yeung 2001; Gibbs, Kraemer, and Dedrick 2003). For instance, Couture et al. (2017) find that, when not accompanied by other complementary interventions to support the transition to local online trading activity, the beneficial side effects of e-commerce are unlikely to materialize in the short to medium run.

## REFERENCES

Bastos Tigre, Paulo, and Jason Dedrick. 2004. "E-Commerce in Brazil: Local Adaptation of a Global Technology." *Electronic Markets* 14 (1): 36–47.

Coppel, Jonathan. 2000. "E-Commerce: Impacts and Policy Challenges." Economics Department Working Paper No. 252, Organisation for Economic Co-operation and Development, Paris.

Couture, V., B. Faber, Y. Gu, and L. Liu. 2017. "E-Commerce Integration and Economic Development." Unpublished paper, Yale University, New Haven, CT.

Efendioglu, Alev M., and Vincent F. Yip. 2004. "Chinese Culture and E-Commerce: An Exploratory Study." *Interacting with Computers* 16 (1): 45–62.

FICCI CMSME (Federation of Indian Chambers of Commerce & Industry—Confederation of Micro, Small, and Medium Enterprises). 2017. "Exploring Potential of E-Commerce for Retail Exports of Indian MSMEs in Manufacturing Sector." Technical Report, Centre for MSME Studies, FICCI CMCME, New Delhi.

Gibbs, Jennifer, Kenneth L. Kraemer, and Jason Dedrick. 2003. "Environment and Policy Factors Shaping Global E-Commerce Diffusion: A Cross-Country Comparison." *Information Society* 19 (1): 5–18.

Goldfarb, Avi, and Catherine Tucker. 2017. "Digital Economics." NBER Working Paper No. 23684, National Bureau of Economic Research, Cambridge, MA.

Goldmanis, Maris, Ali Hortaçsu, Chad Syverson, and Önsel Emre. 2010. "E-Commerce and the Market Structure of Retail Industries." *Economic Journal* 120 (545): 651–82.

Hagiu, Andrei. 2012. "Software Platforms." In *Oxford Handbook of the Digital Economy*, edited by Martin Peitz and Joel Waldfogel, 59–82. New York: Oxford University Press.

IAMAI and Kantar IMRB (Internet and Mobile Association of India and Kantar IMRB). 2016. "Digital Commerce 2016." IAMAI and Kantar IMRB, Delhi.

Jullien, B. 2012. "Two-Sided B to B Platforms." In *Oxford Handbook of the Digital Economy*, edited by Martin Peitz and Joel Waldfogel, 161–85. New York: Oxford University Press.

Kshetri, Nir. 2007. "Barriers to E-Commerce and Competitive Business Models in Developing Countries: A Case-Study." *Electronic Commerce Research and Applications* 6 (4): 443–52.

Nocke, Volker, Martin Peitz, and Konrad Stahl. 2007. "Platform Ownership." *Journal of the European Economic Association* 5 (6): 1130–60.

OECD (Organisation for Economic Co-operation and Development). 2017. "Measuring Digital Trade: Towards a Conceptual Framework." STD/CSSP/WPTGS (2017) 3. Working Party on International Trade in Goods and Trade in Services Statistics, OECD, Paris.

Oxley, Joanne E., and Bernard Yeung. 2001. "E-Commerce Readiness: Institutional Environment and International Competitiveness." *Journal of International Business Studies* 32 (4): 705–23.

Shih, Chuan-Fong, Jason Dedrick, and Kenneth L. Kraemer. 2005. "Rule of Law and the International Diffusion of E-Commerce." *Communications of the Association for Computing Machinery* 48 (11): 57–62.

# 2 Constraints on E-Commerce
## RESULTS FROM THE E-COMMERCE DEVELOPMENT SURVEY

For this study, a survey of more than 2,200 firms in South Asia was conducted in 2018, to understand broad trends in and constraints on e-commerce. The survey was done in partnership with Nextrade Group.[1] The South Asia survey was conducted from March to May 2018 and covered 1,688 merchants in nine major sectors, plus 539 e-commerce ecosystem firms (such as e-commerce and payment platforms and logistics, financial services, and information technology services firms) that service merchants across seven economies (Afghanistan, Bangladesh, Bhutan, India, Nepal, Pakistan, and Sri Lanka). The random sample was constructed in two ways: about two-thirds of the respondents responded to an online survey, and the remaining one-third responded to a computer-assisted telephone interview.

In the region, 31 percent of the surveyed firms reported selling and buying online, 27 percent reported only selling online, 10 percent reported only buying online, and about 31 percent reported neither selling nor buying online (figure 2.1). Online sales activity appears to be somewhat correlated with firm size, with large firms (defined by the survey as those with more than 250 employees) being more likely to sell online than their smaller counterparts.

The surveyed companies that reported online sales (that is, those that sell online or sell and buy online) are much more internationalized than those that neither buy nor sell goods or services online. For example, while only 17 percent of small South Asian companies that do not have online sales or purchases report any export activity, 48 percent of small companies that do sell and buy online report export activity (figure 2.2). Moreover, online sellers are more diversified in their export markets than offline sellers: while offline sellers sell mostly to their domestic market or to one or two export markets, around 40 percent of online sellers cater to more than three foreign markets. Online traders also seem more likely to grow fast: 33 percent of the surveyed online sellers saw revenue growth of 10 percent or higher in 2016–17, whereas only 21 percent of the interviewees reported this type of revenue growth among offline sellers.

The most frequently cited challenges to the adoption of e-commerce, among the surveyed South Asian firms that did not report any online sales, include concerns about the cost of selling online, together with uncertainty about the resulting return on investment. In addition, these firms often mentioned inadequate connectivity and information technology (IT) infrastructure as substantial hurdles preventing their online activity.

**FIGURE 2.1**

## Surveyed firms, by online activity

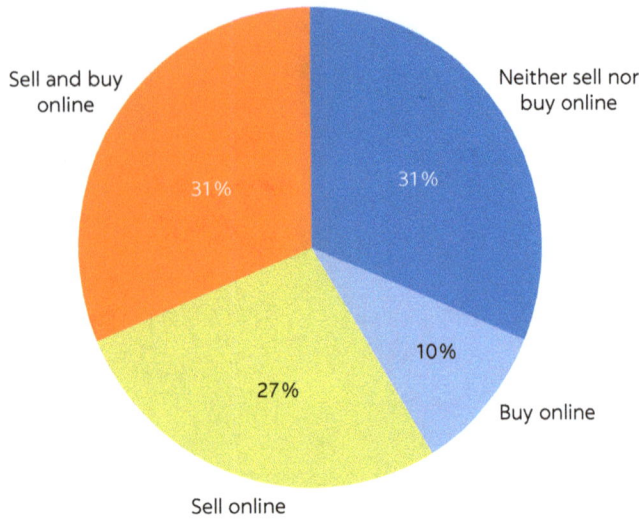

*Source:* Computer-assisted telephone interviews, Nextrade Group.
*Note:* Totals may not add to 100 because of rounding.

Logistics, digital regulations, and connectivity are cited as the main challenges among online sellers, including both large and small firms, whereas online payments, e-commerce logistics, connectivity, and IT infrastructure appear to be significant constraints for small firms in particular (figure 2.3).

Much of the South Asian firms' international e-trade tends to be with extraregional partners, such as China, the United Kingdom, and the United States. Within international or cross-border e-commerce, the key obstacles are logistics (such as clearing customs for e-commerce imports and exports) and connectivity and digital regulations in other countries (figure 2.4). Compared with exporters, nonexporters also report being concerned about their own capabilities for doing cross-border e-commerce and about access to trade finance.

These assessments vary quite significantly across countries. For example, small sellers in Afghanistan are particularly constrained by access to trade finance, while firms in Pakistan and Bangladesh cite connectivity and IT backbone as significant hurdles for cross-border e-commerce. Digital regulations appear to be a concern for firms in all countries (figure 2.5).

**FIGURE 2.2**

## Percentage of South Asian companies that export, by size and online activity

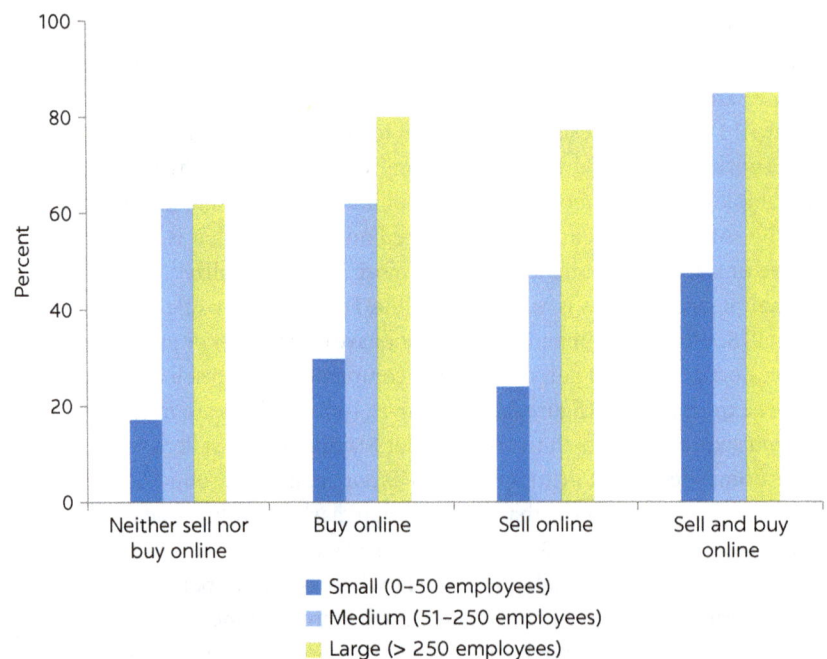

*Source:* Computer-assisted telephone interviews, Nextrade Group.

**FIGURE 2.3**

## Online sellers' ratings of the enabling environment for domestic e-commerce sales

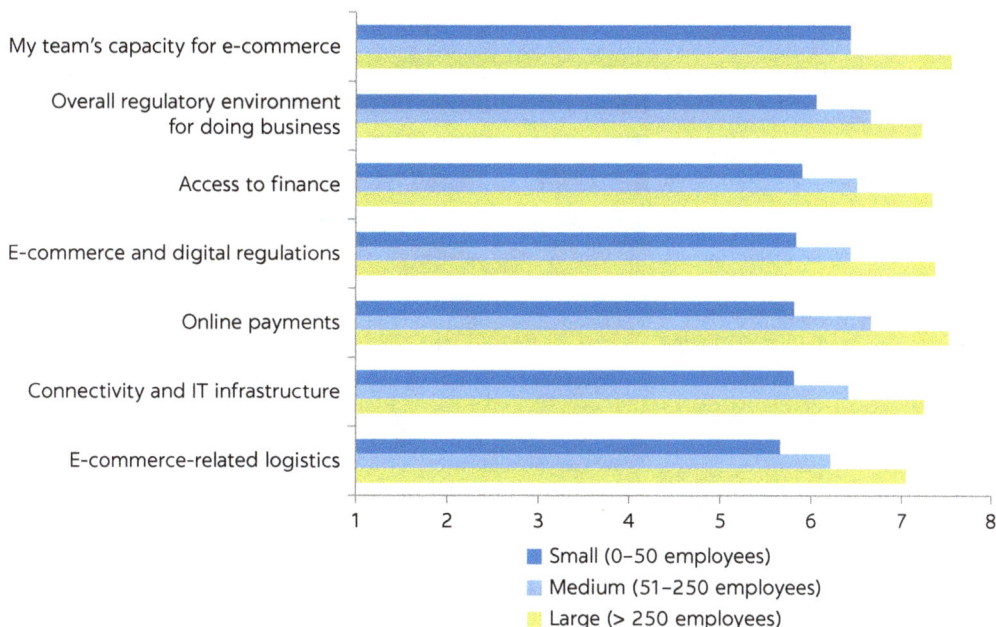

Source: Computer-assisted telephone interviews, Nextrade Group.
Note: 1 = very poor; 10 = excellent. IT = information technology.

**FIGURE 2.4**

## Online sellers' ratings of the enabling environment for cross-border e-commerce sales

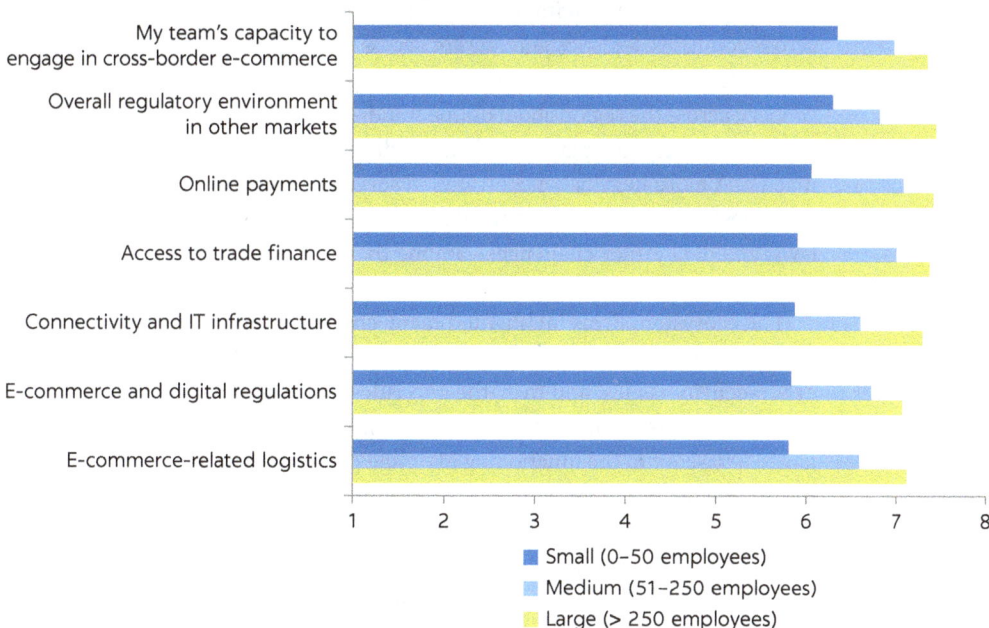

Source: Computer-assisted telephone interviews, Nextrade Group.
Note: 1 = very poor; 10 = excellent. IT = information technology.

**FIGURE 2.5**

## Small online sellers' ratings of the enabling environment for cross-border e-commerce sales, by country

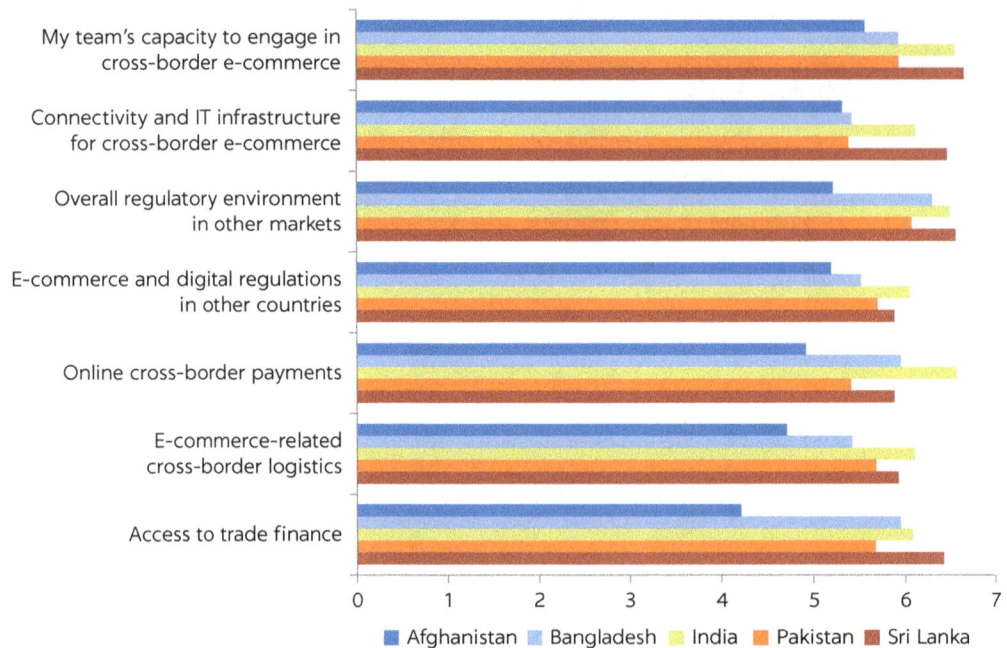

*Source:* Computer-assisted telephone interviews, Nextrade Group.
*Note:* 1 = very poor; 10 = excellent. IT = information technology.

Small South Asian online sellers are especially concerned about the cost of logistics to the end buyer, the complexities of customs clearance, the functioning of online payments, and basic digital infrastructure such as the cost of broadband and the population's digital literacy. Although the challenges vary somewhat across countries, logistics and market access and online payment issues appear to trouble small online sellers in each economy. Furthermore, there appears to be concern across the region about online fraud—such as with counterparties' identities, data piracy, and payments fraud. Indian firms, which tend to be more digitized and more heavily concentrated in service sectors than firms in the other countries, tended to highlight regulatory issues—such as tax rules, legal liability laws, and data piracy challenges—among their top challenges to engaging with e-commerce.

The ecosystem firms highlighted many challenges arising from digital regulatory issues as well. These include online Internet portal protection rules, cybersecurity issues, and over-the-top rules, such as the application of rigid broadcast and telecom rules on Internet intermediaries. Ecosystem firms also gave a low score to the functioning of online payments and merchants' capabilities to engage in e-commerce. Digital illiteracy and digital identity concerns were highlighted as substantial challenges by merchants and ecosystem firms.

Cross-border e-commerce faces many hurdles. Firms in Afghanistan, Bangladesh, India, Nepal, and Pakistan all rated the cost of cross-border logistics as being among their top 10 specific hurdles, while firms in Afghanistan, India, Pakistan, and Sri Lanka said that taxes and trade barriers in export markets are among their main challenges (table 2.1).

If their top three e-commerce problems were resolved, South Asian firms expect substantial benefits in exports, employment, and production growth (figure 2.6). For example, Pakistani firms expect to grow their exports by

TABLE 2.1 **Small online sellers' priority challenges in cross-border e-commerce**

| | SOUTH ASIA | AFGHANISTAN | BANGLADESH | INDIA | NEPAL | PAKISTAN | SRI LANKA |
|---|---|---|---|---|---|---|---|
| Overall cost of cross-border logistics | 1 | 1 | 4 | 3 | 7 | 4 | 21 |
| Customs clearance of low-value shipments | 2 | 8 | 18 | 1 | 2 | 13 | 14 |
| Customs rules on low-value shipments | 3 | 9 | 12 | 4 | 1 | 11 | 8 |
| Taxes or trade barriers in export markets | 4 | 10 | 9 | 2 | 17 | 3 | 10 |
| Customs procedures for e-commerce imports | 5 | 5 | 2 | 9 | 12 | 12 | 18 |
| Tariffs in export markets | 6 | 20 | 7 | 5 | 10 | 6 | 23 |
| Total cost of delivery from my country to foreign customer | 7 | 2 | 10 | 11 | 3 | 23 | 6 |
| Infrastructure for cross-border e-commerce | 8 | 7 | 11 | 7 | 13 | 5 | 25 |
| Local content requirements | 9 | 15 | 8 | 15 | 9 | 2 | 7 |
| Customs procedures for my e-commerce exports in main export markets | 10 | 13 | 1 | 12 | 6 | 22 | 22 |
| Postal services for cross-border e-commerce—import or export | 11 | 3 | 5 | 13 | 14 | 15 | 24 |
| Forex restrictions—cross-border payments | 12 | 22 | 14 | 18 | 4 | 8 | 16 |
| Cost of cross-border online payments | 13 | 21 | 13 | 17 | 5 | 7 | 15 |
| IP protections in other markets | 14 | 16 | 15 | 16 | 19 | 9 | 3 |
| Compliance with health, safety, environmental, and product standards | 15 | 17 | 3 | 20 | 20 | 17 | 19 |

*Source:* Computer-assisted telephone interviews, Nextrade Group.
*Note:* Darker cells and smaller numbers indicate higher priorities. Forex = foreign exchange; IP = Internet protocol.

FIGURE 2.6

**South Asian firms' estimated gains if the top three challenges in e-commerce were removed**

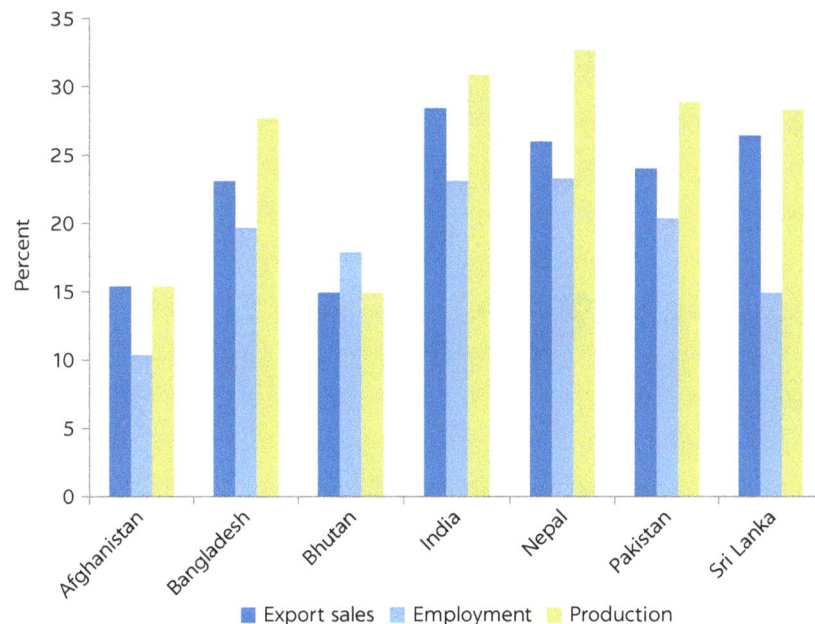

*Source:* Computer-assisted telephone interviews, Nextrade Group.

23 percent and employment by 20 percent if their top barriers to e-commerce were removed. The gains are similar across firms of all sizes and tend to be higher in countries with a larger share of online sellers.

## NOTE

1. The Global E-Commerce Development survey was developed by the Nextrade Group in 2015–16 and funded as a pilot by the U.S. Agency for International Development. The survey has now been expanded by the World Bank Group to several regions.

# 3 Eliminating Transaction Costs through E-Commerce

## POLICIES AT THE NATIONAL LEVEL

Appropriate regulations can help unleash the potential of e-commerce to reduce transaction costs. Regulatory hurdles that businesses face when engaging in e-commerce can relate to five focus areas: (a) consumer protection, (b) data protection and privacy, (c) e-transactions and e-signatures, (d) cybersecurity,[1] and (e) market access and investment-related policy measures. The presence or absence and quality of these regulations can shape in various ways the ability of e-commerce to reduce transaction costs. Moreover, the lack of a clear regulatory framework is critically constraining e-commerce, not just in South Asia (at the national and intraregional levels), but globally as well. For example, the European Commission attributes the slow pace of online transactions to the complicated and unclear regulatory framework.[2] Private sector consultations in Nepal and Sri Lanka also pointed to the lack of clarity in regulations that leaves young entrepreneurs in "gray" areas, who are later identified as noncompliant.

Consumer protection directly affects search costs on digital platforms, considering the asymmetric information between seller and buyer on the products and services being sold online. This asymmetry of information requires greater responsibilities on the part of the seller, such as the provision of warranties and refund arrangements. Online transactions also have legal uncertainty in enforcement and the relevant jurisdiction for consumer complaints. And digital commerce is more prone to fraud and deception. Effective protection of consumers' rights is critical for the development of e-commerce. Because consumers cannot physically examine the products, they are unsure of the quality of their purchases, which makes the return policy an important factor in their online purchase decisions. At the same time, an excessive regulatory burden can inhibit entry by small enterprises into this market. For instance, the adoption of the "country-of-destination" principle (which allows international consumers to rely on the consumer protection granted to them by their domestic law) could be a counterproductive approach when consumer protection standards are quite heterogeneous across countries.

When it comes to contracting costs, regulation of electronic transactions and signatures and data privacy is paramount. Given the paperless nature of e-transactions, it is crucial to find mechanisms for the identification of parties and the authentication of commercial transactions. In this sense, a central issue is the legal recognition of electronic and digital signatures, so that both parties can be assured of the validity of their transaction. Establishing the full validity of transactions and signatures performed online, however, requires the collection of a large amount of personal data, whose treatment in turn involves delicate trade-offs. On the one hand, consumers are reluctant to engage in online transactions if they are uncertain about the confidentiality of their data. On the other hand, excessively rigid data protection standards are likely to cause frictions in the e-commerce space and may create restrictions on market access.

The lack of or inadequate enforcement of rules on electronic payments deters the potential of e-commerce to abate payment costs. Anonymity and the paperless nature of transactions performed over the Internet require a legal status through a solid base of legitimacy and credibility (Pappas 2002). Digital transaction laws on e-signatures and payment solutions can provide exactly this legitimacy.[3] Specific e-payment regulations are needed to limit legal uncertainties and account for new technologies and e-payment alternatives to cards.[4] These challenges could be addressed when payment mechanisms, such as that offered by PayPal, are allowed to emerge or when transactions are conducted with firms that are highly sensitive about their reputation. Nonetheless, if these mechanisms are not automatic or regulations inhibit the entry of firms such as PayPal, then it may be worthwhile to explore mechanisms for the identification of parties and authentication of commercial transactions. In this sense, the legal recognition of electronic and digital signatures could become a critical issue such that both parties in a transaction can be assured that the validity of their interaction is not hampered by its paperless form. In addition, there is also the need to strengthen regulatory symmetry between financial institutions and other payment agents, to foster a level playing field and a competitive environment for e-payment providers (Olsen et al. 2015).

Cybercrime is of growing concern to countries at all levels of development and affects buyers and sellers. Cybercrime broadly includes hacking, data damages, stolen funds, theft of intellectual property, and theft of data (USITC 2017). In 2012, an estimated US$3.5 billion was lost in supplier revenue because of online fraud (CyberSource 2013). As a result, governments require that the information technology (IT) systems used by their citizens are secure, and that governments are introducing various forms of regulation to ensure that data and digitally supported services have adequate levels of protection. This is particularly relevant for broad certification requirements, encryption regulation, content control, and intellectual property rights law.

Finally, delivery, tax, and regulatory compliance costs are determined by market access and investment restriction measures. Market access regulations can further constrain the development of e-commerce. For example, regulations relating to low thresholds for de minimis, additional compliance burdens on foreign firms, or the taxation of e-commerce sales on the basis of arbitrary rules can have a severe impact on investment in digital services (USITC 2017). In addition, there could be restrictions on the delivery methods, such as local ownership of logistics providers, or on the flexibility allowed to such providers. All these measures increase the cost of doing business internationally and predictably result in distorted business flows and lost market opportunities. Appropriate e-commerce regulations, if instituted and implemented, may help circumvent these barriers.

## CONSUMER PROTECTION

Consumer protection regulations make provisions for respecting consumers' rights and penalize fraudulent business practices. Considering the extent of information asymmetry that exists between sellers and buyers on the Internet, consumers are particularly vulnerable to deceptive and fraudulent activities when purchasing goods or services online. Therefore, consumer protection laws are meant to limit as far as possible the exposure of consumers to misleading, fraudulent, and unfair commercial practices. This is achieved by clarifying the requirements of doing business online within a particular jurisdiction for businesses engaged in e-commerce, or by providing consumers with effective redress mechanisms, or again by empowering them through awareness, education, and training in IT skills (European Commission 2016; UNCTAD 2013b, 2015a).

Consumer protection regulations help identify online sellers, through registration rules or enforcement of certain technology (for example, encryption). The requirement that evidence of any transaction be provided, or that consumers' consent be explicitly sought in relation to potentially harmful contract clauses,[5] are meaningful examples of attempts at limiting the adverse effects of information asymmetries (Binding and Purnhagen 2011; Kilic and Israel 2015; UNCTAD 2015b). Such regulations are also critical for the development of businesses' self-regulatory systems (OECD 2000). Although self-regulation alone has been deemed insufficient to provide adequate consumer protection (Budnitz 1998), various countries, like China or the United States, have supervised and supported the establishment of industry self-regulation and codes of conduct, together with the activities of consumer organizations (Binding and Purnhagen 2011; Boritz and No 2011).[6] This report acknowledges that consumer protection may not be central to the constraints crippling the growth of e-commerce in South Asia, where firms with reputational capital may offer credible forms of consumer protection, going beyond legal norms.

Homogenizing international consumer protection frameworks can potentially encourage higher participation in e-commerce. Studies suggest that the many different levels of consumer protection distort cross-border competition in European Union member states and create incentives for producers and consumers to transact in their home markets. Yet, businesses operating in various countries can benefit from a one-stop-shop approach, whereby it becomes simpler, faster, and cheaper to resolve consumer issues (European Commission 2016). Moreover, consistent cross-border enforcement of consumer legislation increases legal certainty and reduces legal costs when implementing marketing on foreign platforms.

## DATA PROTECTION AND PRIVACY

Data privacy regulations offer individuals the right to control their personal information. This right covers various aspects of personal information with respect to its collection, use, and transfer by entities engaged in e-commerce (Boritz and No 2011). In a digital commerce setting, privacy is violated whenever personal information that can be linked to an individual or used to identify an individual is collected, used, or transferred without authorization, as a direct result of an e-commerce transaction (Milberg, Smith, and Burke 2000;

Petty 2000; Rezgui, Bouguettaya, and Eltoweissy 2003). Where data protection regulations are in place, any transaction or online activity involving the transfer of sensitive information (including the collection of browsing history data using so-called "web cookies")[7] becomes subject to scrutiny to avoid any unauthorized breach of individual privacy.[8]

Data protection practices should be inspired by a set of core principles (UNCTAD 2016). To begin, organizations engaging in e-commerce should openly disclose their personal data policies. Then, the collection of personal data must be limited, lawful, and fair, and consumers must be aware of it and explicitly give their consent. The purpose of collection and (eventual) disclosure of personal data must in any case be specified at the time of collection, and data use or disclosure must be limited to the purposes specified or to closely related purposes. The "data minimization" principle in addition requires that data not directly relevant to the purpose of collection are not collected. Furthermore, the collected personal data must be subject to appropriate security safeguards and be relevant, accurate, and up-to-date—which also means that data subjects must have appropriate rights to access and correct their personal data. Finally, data controllers must take responsibility for ensuring compliance with the data protection principles.

Data privacy regulation requires a delicate balance between adequate levels of protection and sufficient degrees of freedom for business activity. This often requires trading off consumer confidence and smooth market operations, at the risk of creating negative market effects either way (UNCTAD 2016; USITC 2013). For example, Graef, Wahyuningtyas, and Valcke (2015) document how, in the case of online platforms, successful companies might foreclose competition by raising barriers to entry in the collection of user data, thereby damaging competitors and new entrants that need access to those data to provide competing or complementary services. New challenges are also posed by recent innovations in information and communications technology (ICT), such as cloud services,[9] the Internet of Things,[10] and big data analytics,[11] which are revolutionizing the way in which social, economic, and financial activities are currently undertaken, but at the same time rely on personal-data-intensive technologies and processes (UNCTAD 2016).

Countries have adopted two distinct approaches to data protection and privacy measures. Countries follow a comprehensive ("omnibus") approach—regulating data flows across all sectors of the economy—or a sectoral approach—applying different regimes to specific industries, such as financial services.[12] Examples of countries applying these approaches are the European Union and the United States, respectively.

Data protection policies in a cross-border context need to be designed carefully so that they do not result in disguised protectionism. The risk of such policies lies in placing international competitors at a disadvantage compared with their domestic counterparts. In various countries, the law mandates that companies maintain privacy policies restricting the processing of sensitive personal data for international transfers, and that foreign companies using domestic data have their computing facilities within the national borders (Kilic and Israel 2015; Swedish National Board of Trade 2012; UNCTAD 2016). In the case of consumer protection, it is not clear that data protection would be foremost among consumer concerns in South Asia; nonetheless, it is an area in which South Asian governments are increasing regulatory oversight.

## E-TRANSACTIONS, DIGITAL SIGNATURES, E-PAYMENTS, AND DISPUTE RESOLUTION

Purchasing online is still not a widespread option in many South Asian countries. Although global online purchases account for about 16 percent of total purchases, and the figure is more than 60 percent in developed markets such as the Republic of Korea and the United States, South Asian countries like Bangladesh stand at only 1 percent. Among various reasons, the anonymity and paperless nature of transactions performed over the Internet seem to constitute a serious obstacle for digital transactions. A survey of Indian consumers revealed that most shoppers look for information online but then purchase the items offline because they need to "touch and feel" the product or they have security concerns (IAMAI and Kantar IMRB 2016). This trust gap can only be filled by building a solid base of legitimacy and credibility for electronic transactions (Pappas 2002).

Digital transaction laws on e-signatures and payment solutions can provide some of this legitimacy.[13] First, specific e-payment regulations are needed to limit legal uncertainties and account for new technologies and e-payment alternatives to credit and debit cards (Miao and Jayakar 2016; Olsen et al. 2015).[14] Olsen et al. (2015) also stress the need to strengthen regulatory symmetry between financial institutions and other payment agents to foster a level playing field and competitive environment for e-payment providers. Then, the priority is to find mechanisms for the identification of parties and the authentication of commercial transactions. In this sense, a central issue is the legal recognition of electronic and digital signatures, so that both parties in a transaction can rest assured that the validity of their interaction is not hampered by its paperless form.

The legal treatment of digital signatures relies on three fundamental components: public key infrastructure technology, the role of certificate authorities, and the choice between technological neutrality and legal specificity (Bhatia 2003). First, the purpose of public key infrastructure is to enable e-commerce participants to authenticate each other, communicate in a confidential way, and provide electronic documents with a legally binding digital signature. Second, the validity and authenticity of the signature are then ensured by the certificate authority, which certifies that a particular public key belongs to the actual sender. Therefore, the establishment of rules for the licensing and recognition of certificate authorities lies at the core of any regulation on digital signatures (Bhatia 2003; Binding and Purnhagen 2011; Murad 2010; Penbera 1999). Third, e-transaction legislation can have various degrees of specificity as to which technologies can be considered valid in the issuance of digital signatures and the respective certificates. A country is technologically neutral when there is no explicit prescription of a particular type of technology; it is legal-specific when there are legally defined, specific public key infrastructure rules (Bhatia 2003).

The treatment of electronic and digital signatures represents a nonnegligible obstacle to cross-border transactions. Different countries follow different legal approaches and require more or less stringent standards for the licensing of certificate authorities or authentication of signatures and notarization of transactions. Consequently, what is perfectly legal in one country might not meet the legal requirements in another, creating additional costs for firms trying to expand their activities abroad (Kilic and Israel 2015; USITC 2013, 2017).

The lack of a systematic dispute resolution mechanism in an international context complicates cross-border trade through e-commerce. UNCTAD (2015a) reports an increasing number of cross-border disputes and fewer case settlements, which calls for the establishment of a coordinated method for resolving online disputes (Olsen et al. 2015). However, apart from notable exceptions like the European Union, there have been very few regional- or international-level facilities to settle cross-border disputes to date. Therefore, disputes are usually dealt with by specific jurisdictions chosen by the parties upon closing a transaction. The agreement on the choice of jurisdiction is a common practice in international contracts, which allows the parties to choose a court (or courts) to settle future disputes, or a dispute that has already taken place. The selected court will have exclusive jurisdiction to decide, unless agreed on otherwise by the parties. In e-commerce contracts, however, jurisdiction clauses are commonly included in the general conditions of contracting, whose acceptance by the end user is often obtained through the click-wrapping technique.[15] As such, the choice of court agreement incorporated into the contract might easily go unnoticed, which raises concerns as to the existence of an actual agreement between the parties (Gonçalves De Sousa 2017).

## CYBERSECURITY

To ensure cybersecurity, countries need to work on critical information infrastructure regulations. These generally include some broad certification requirements, such as yearly certification processes and attestations (Friedman 2013). Some countries at the extreme end of the spectrum demand full access not just to the products or software, but also to the underlying source code. That has recently been the case for Brazil, China, and Indonesia, which required source code disclosure to relevant government authorities as a prerequisite for firms to operate within their borders (USITC 2017). Clearly, source code may not be securely stored everywhere, giving rise to risks of intellectual property rights infringement. Consequently, it is often the case that firms shy away from certain industries and countries, and that cybersecurity regulations may result in (only to an extent) trade restrictions.

Encryption regulations are also critical for ensuring cybersecurity.[16] Encryption enables users to protect the confidentiality of their data and communications. Restrictions on encryption use imposed—for example, by China, India, or the United Kingdom—are rationalized on the grounds that they reduce the risk of transmission of information that may enable harmful activities. However, inadequate standards pose a risk of reducing the security and privacy of digital goods. For instance, USITC (2017) reports that India's encryption regulations require firms to use a 40-bit or lower standard encryption to secure digitally transmitted information, while most U.S. firms are using stronger standards (ranging from 128-bit to 256-bit). Therefore, digital trade between the United States and India requires that U.S. firms procure a license to use their (more sophisticated and secure) cryptography standards with Indian businesses or consumers.

Content control is also often justified on the grounds of cybersecurity. Content control is the outright blocking or filtering by governments of their Internet platforms and content. As for other instances of cybersecurity regulation, the enactment of such actions may well be justified by overarching principles, such as the need for protection of national security, public order, or human life. For instance, various European countries (including France, Italy, and the United Kingdom) block websites that promote terrorism or child pornography. However, incidents of outright censorship are becoming increasingly common and usually impose costs on the economies of the countries implementing them. On the basis of an analysis of 81 short-term Internet shutdowns in 19 countries, West (2016) estimates that shutdowns resulted in at least US$2.4 billion in forgone world gross domestic product (GDP) in 2015 and 2016.

Violation of intellectual property rights (online piracy) is ever more pervasive. Online piracy of television episodes and movies, for example, is estimated to have cost the global content industry US$32 billion in 2017, and this is forecast to grow to US$52 billion in lost revenue by 2022 (FICCI and EY 2018). Other than contributing to innovation, creativity, and commerce, the access to large amounts of content granted by the Internet to potentially every broadband user has led to large-scale abuses of intellectual property rights, which can occur through a variety of means and devices. Instances of intellectual property rights violations include the infringement of patents, copyrights, and author rights, as well as the unauthorized sale of franchise goods, counterfeit or smuggled goods, and the misuse of brands and trademarks (Binding and Purnhagen 2011; Primo Braga 2005; UNCTAD 2017a, 2017b). USITC (2013) also identifies unauthorized software installation onto PCs, mobile devices, and media boxes,[17] and end-user software piracy as examples of the same.[18] Other digital-era-specific examples are cybersquatting[19] and the misuse of website and domain names (Binding and Purnhagen 2011; UNCTAD 2015b).

In India, the film industry alone is estimated to lose US$2.8 billion of its total revenue to piracy every year, but piracy rates may be even higher for other types of content (FICCI and EY 2018). Revenue leakages for Indian films may be around 10–30 percent of revenue, and losses may be even higher for music, software, and games.[20] The content industry is also reported to suffer substantially from piracy, especially the illegal sharing of local television programming (Liang and Sundaram 2011) and streaming of sport matches (FICCI and EY 2018). Moreover, the globalization of Bollywood and the large Indian diaspora have helped to make film and content piracy an international business. Indian tracker sites receive substantial shares of their traffic from Bangladesh, Pakistan, and Sri Lanka, as well as from Australia, Canada, Dubai, Qatar, the United Kingdom, and the United States (Liang and Sundaram 2011). Deloitte (2016) further reports that, among the more than 150 websites offering pirated versions of Indian films, almost two-thirds are located abroad.

A strong legal framework and effective enforcement mechanisms could combat online piracy. The extent to which these conditions are met in different countries crucially determines the profitability of cross-border activities. For example, in the United States, focus group representatives of the content industries[21] identified Internet piracy as the single most important barrier to digital trade for their industries (USITC 2013). In particular, the Office of the U.S. Trade Representative (USTR 2016) estimates the value of losses to U.S. producers from piracy of music and movies in India at around US$4 billion per year, and the commercial value of unlicensed software used in India at about US$3 billion. Moreover, controversies often arise as to the liability of Internet service providers (ISPs) for providing bona fide access to copyright-infringing content (USITC 2017). ISPs lament regulations that are too stringent that hold them accountable for providing transient or incidental access in which the access is not expressly prohibited by the copyright holder; however, many judicial and regulatory systems have been shifting the burden to ISPs to monitor their content.[22] Given the above, cybercrime presents complicated enforcement and jurisdictional problems and demands greater international cooperation in the context of cross-border interactions (UNCTAD 2015a).

## MARKET ACCESS REGULATIONS

Specific market access regulations for e-commerce can play a critical role in promoting healthy competition between domestic and foreign businesses (OECD 2017). For instance, many cross-border packages are likely the result of direct business-to-consumer (B2C) online transactions. Low de minimis limits, which require exporters to pay customs duties and taxes and comply with standard customs procedures for shipments above a certain threshold, can distort competition for e-commerce retailers. Low thresholds act as a significant obstacle to cross-border transactions, especially in the context of small-scale online retail purchases, whose cost and processing times can increase significantly because they pay a fixed and a variable cost over every low-value transaction. This burden is further exacerbated by a distinct lack of transparency from many customs agencies about the compliance process, which can differ significantly from destination to destination (USITC 2013).

"Geo-blocking" presents another practical barrier to e-trade (European Commission 2016; Kilic and Israel 2015). Geo-blocking refers to practices that result in the denial of access to websites from other countries, or in the inability to access products or services for sale on those websites (for example, because payment is only accepted if made with a credit card from a certain country). The European Commission (2016) points out how these practices equally affect consumers and businesses as end users of products and services.

Measures that favor domestic industry at the expense of foreign competitors, so-called localization barriers, also constitute a constraint on market access (Stone, Messent, and Flaig 2015). Localization barriers can manifest in the form of local content requirements, such as mandatory national sourcing of goods or services. Audiovisual quotas, for example, place limits on the number of foreign films that can enter the market, cap the percent of time that radio or television stations can play foreign content, or set a minimum play time for domestically produced content (USTR 2013). USITC (2013) notes that, as people consume more media online, these requirements are expanding into trade in digital products—such as movies, music, and e-books—to the detriment of companies selling their content in foreign markets.

Regulations that require foreign companies to adopt local standards restrict entry in the digital space. These regulations often comprise complying with country- or region-specific technical standards or carrying out unnecessary, duplicative conformity assessment procedures in the country where firms operate. Discriminatory regulations that impose country-specific technical standards or local testing requirements on hardware and software products raise the costs of new technologies for consumers and businesses and can seriously limit firms' ability to sell digital products across borders (USITC 2017).

Regulations can also specifically target foreign direct investment (FDI). Foreign ownership rules can establish an equity cap for foreign equity participation or mandate joint ventures with domestic partners, which often requires a transfer of technology to the host country. For example, foreign ownership in all telecom services in Brazil is capped at 49 percent, and China requires that majority ownership in cloud computing be held by a local joint venture (USITC 2017). In India, 100 percent foreign investment in business-to-business e-commerce is permitted; however, the multibrand B2C segment is subject to many restrictions, including FDI not being permitted in the inventory-based model of e-commerce. Other, more subtle barriers to entry are onerous licensing and capital requirements, large fees, and burdensome approval processes that target foreign entities. For instance, Indonesia has proposed to require foreign IT service providers to set up an affiliate in Indonesia to do business in the country, with a process that would entail burdensome registration with the IT regulator and the Investment Coordinating Board (USITC 2017).

The taxation of e-commerce poses several challenges as well. High e-commerce import taxes serve the double purpose of shielding domestic industries from competition (USITC 2017) and providing a significant source of tariff revenue (Bastos Tigre and O'Connor 2002). Governments have various degrees of freedom in shaping their e-commerce tax framework (Primo Braga 2005). First, because soft goods (for example, software, books, and music) can be classified as goods or services, the definition of digital goods is a nontrivial point, especially if services are not taxed in the relevant tax jurisdiction. Similarly, the characterization of income generated by e-commerce (business profits or royalty income) has implications for income tax collection. Furthermore, the definition of "place of permanent establishment" for e-commerce enterprises has implications for indirect tax and income tax: for instance, a firm may have a website hosted by a local ISP despite being physically based abroad, but local authorities could tax sales associated with that website if having the local website qualifies as evidence of permanent establishment (Bastos Tigre and O'Connor 2002; Primo Braga 2005).

## NOTES

1. Inter alia, this label also encompasses intellectual content regulation, domain name regulation, and property rights protection.
2. In the European Union, only 15 percent of consumers buy online from another EU country and 8 percent of firms sell cross-border. As part of its efforts to unlock the potential of e-commerce, the European Commission has adopted a package of proposals to improve the enforcement of consumers' rights, stop unjustified geo-blocking, and increase the transparency of parcel delivery prices.
3. An electronic signature can take the form of a digital signature, a scanned image of a handwritten signature, a digitized fingerprint, a retinal scan, a personal identification number, or even just a name typed at the end of an e-mail (Murad 2010). A digital signature is created and verified by using cryptography, and it is therefore the most secure form of electronic signature.
4. See, for example, Miao and Jayakar (2016) and Olsen et al. (2015). Examples are popular platforms like Alipay, Amazon Payments, and PayPal, and mobile money (m-payments), which allows buyers to perform payments through their mobile device (mobile phone, smartphone, or tablet), taking advantage of mobile telecommunications networks or proximity technologies (Dahlberg et al. 2008).

5. Opt-in rather than opt-out campaigns and regulation of unsolicited online advertising.

6. Under the industry self-regulation approach, each company is responsible for deciding on the degree of information that is collected and used and developing its own privacy policy statement aligned with its industry guidelines (Boritz and No 2011). In China, for example, the self-discipline and self-regulation practices of e-commerce trade associations and public media supervision are important complements to governmental regulation (Binding and Purnhagen 2011).

7. A cookie is a message given to a web browser by a web server. The message is then stored by the browser in a text file and sent back to the server each time the browser requests a page from that server. Cookies are used to identify users and possibly prepare customized web pages for them, including targeted advertising.

8. See Caudill and Murphy (2000); Graef, Wahyuningtyas, and Valcke (2015); Jamal, Maier, and Sunder (2003); Johnson-Page and Thatcher (2001); Milberg, Smith, and Burke (2000); Penbera (1999); Rizzi (2002); and Smith (2001).

9. Cloud services are provided to and used by clients via on-demand, self-service provisioning and administration, through any access network, using any connected devices that use compatible technologies (UNCTAD 2013a).

10. The Internet of Things is the network of physical devices, vehicles, home appliances, and other items embedded with electronics, software, sensors, actuators, and network connectivity that enable these objects to send and receive data.

11. Big data analytics is a methodology that enables the analysis of growing volumes of structured transaction data, plus other forms of semistructured and unstructured data, whose potential is often left untapped by conventional business intelligence and analytics programs.

12. See, for example, Littler and Hudson (2004) on the regulation of online platforms for financial services.

13. An electronic signature can take the form of a digital signature, a scanned image of a handwritten signature, a digitized fingerprint, a retinal scan, a personal identification number, or even just a name typed at the end of an e-mail (Murad 2010). A digital signature is created and verified by using cryptography and is therefore the most secure form of electronic signature.

14. Examples are popular platforms like Alipay, Amazon Payments, and PayPal, and mobile money (m-payments), which allow buyers to perform payments through their mobile device (mobile phone, smartphone, or tablet), taking advantage of mobile telecommunications networks or proximity technologies (Dahlberg et al. 2008).

15. Most click-wrap agreements require end users to manifest their assent by clicking an "OK" or "Agree" button on a dialog box or pop-up window. Rejection is instead manifested by clicking "Cancel" or closing the pop-up window and results in the inability on the part of the end user to use or purchase the product or service.

16. See the policy brief on encryption by the Internet Society (2016).

17. Manufacturers and dealers install illegal copies of software, movies, music, television programming, and other creative materials on Internet-connected devices.

18. These include the installation of software on multiple computers beyond the terms of a license, as well as client-server overuse, in which more than the authorized number of employees have access to a program.

19. Cybersquatting is the registration of, trafficking in, or use of an Internet domain name that corresponds to another brand or a famous individual, with bad faith intent to profit from the goodwill of a trademark belonging to someone else. The cybersquatter then offers to sell the domain to the person or company that owns a trademark contained within the name at an inflated price (U.S. Anticybersquatting Consumer Protection Act, 1999, 15 USC §1125(D)).

20. In 2009, the piracy rates for music, software, and games in the online space were estimated at 99, 65, and 90 percent of the Indian market, respectively (BSA and IDC 2010; IIPA 2009).

21. These include software, music, movies, books and journals, and video games.

22. In India, for example, in the case of *Star India Pvt. Ltd v. Haneeth Ujwal*, the Delhi High Court held that ISPs are obliged to ensure that third-party intellectual property rights are not violated through their networks (Intellectual Property Watch 2014). USITC (2017) reports that, although Indian courts are imposing civil sanctions on intermediaries that fail to manage copyright protections on their website, they have not yet imposed criminal sanctions.

## REFERENCES

Bastos Tigre, Paulo, and Jason Dedrick. 2004. "E-Commerce in Brazil: Local Adaptation of a Global Technology." *Electronic Markets* 14 (1): 36–47.

Bastos Tigre, Paulo, and David O'Connor. 2002. "Policies and Institutions for E-Commerce Readiness: What Can Developing Countries Learn from OECD Experience?" Working Paper 189, OECD Development Centre, Paris.

Bhatia, S. 2003. *Analysis of Electronic Commerce: Regulation in the Global Economy*. Honors thesis, Ohio State University, Columbus.

Binding, Jörg, and Kai Purnhagen. 2011. "Regulations on E-Commerce Consumer Protection Rules in China and Europe Compared—Same Same but Different? *Journal of Intellectual Property, Information Technology and Electronic Commerce Law* 4: 186–94.

Boritz, J. Efrim, and Won Gyun No. 2011. "E-Commerce and Privacy: Exploring What We Know and Opportunities for Future Discovery." *Journal of Information Systems* 25 (2): 11–45.

BSA and IDC (Business Software Alliance and International Data Corporation). 2010. *2009 Global Software Piracy Study*. Washington, DC: BSA and IDC.

Budnitz, Mark E. 1998. "Privacy Protection for Consumer Transactions in Electronic Commerce: Why Self-Regulation Is Inadequate." *South Carolina Law Review* 49: 847–86.

Caudill, Eve M., and Patrick E. Murphy. 2000. "Consumer Online Privacy: Legal and Ethical Issues." *Journal of Public Policy and Marketing* 19 (1): 7–19.

CyberSource. 2013. *Online Fraud Report: Online Payment Fraud Trends, Merchant Practices, and Benchmarks*. 14th annual edition. Foster City, CA: CyberSource Corporation.

Dahlberg, Tomi, Niina Mallat, Jan Ondrus, and Agnieszka Zmijewska. 2008. "Past, Present and Future of Mobile Payments Research: A Literature Review." *Electronic Commerce Research and Applications* 7 (2): 165–81.

Deloitte. 2016. *Indywood: The Indian Film Industry*. Technical report. Mumbai: Deloitte Touche Tohmatsu India LLP.

European Commission. 2016. "Questions and Answers: Boosting E-Commerce in the EU." Communication IP/16/1887, Press Release Database, European Commission, Brussels, May 25.

FICCI and EY (Federation of Indian Chambers of Commerce & Industry and Ernst and Young). 2018. "Re-Imagining India's M&E Sector." Technical Report, FICCI and Ernst and Young LLP, New Delhi.

Friedman, Allan A. 2013. "Cybersecurity and Trade: National Policies, Global and Local Consequences." Report of the Center for Technology Innovations, Brookings Institution, Washington, DC.

Gonçalves De Sousa, A. S. 2017. "Choice-of-Court Agreements in the E-Commerce International Contracts." *Masaryk University Journal of Law and Technology* 11 (1): 63–76.

Graef, Inge, Sih Y. Wahyuningtyas, and Peggy Valcke. 2015. "Assessing Data Access Issues in Online Platforms." *Telecommunications Policy* 39 (5): 375–87.

IAMAI and Kantar IMRB (Internet and Mobile Association of India and Kantar IMRB). 2016. "Digital Commerce 2016." IAMAI and Kantar IMRB, Delhi.

IIPA (International Intellectual Property Alliance). 2009. *India: IIPA Special 301 Report on Copyright Protection and Enforcement, 2009*. Washington, DC: IIPA.

Intellectual Property Watch. 2014. *Inside Views: The Indian Copyright (Amendment) Act*. Geneva: Intellectual Property Watch.

Internet Society. 2016. "Policy Brief: Encryption." Internet Society, Reston, VA. https://www .internetsociety.org/policybriefs/encryption/.

Jamal, Karim, Michael Maier, and Shyam Sunder. 2003. "Privacy in E-Commerce: Development of Reporting Standards, Disclosure, and Assurance Services in an Unregulated Market." *Journal of Accounting Research* 41 (2): 285–309.

Johnson-Page, Grace F., and R. Scott Thatcher. 2001. "B2C Data Privacy Policies: Current Trends." *Management Decision* 39 (4): 261–71.

Kilic, Burcu, and Tamir Israel. 2015. *The Highlights of the Trans-Pacific Partnership E-commerce Chapter*. Ottawa: Canadian Internet Policy and Public Interest Clinic at the University of Ottawa Faculty of Law.

Liang, Lawrence, and R. Sundaram. 2011. "India." In *Media Piracy in Emerging Economies*, edited by Joe Karaganis, chapter 8. New York: Social Science Research Council.

Littler, Kevin, and Robert Hudson. 2004. "The Impact of Depolarisation on E-Commerce Development in the Distribution of Regulated Financial Products." *International Journal of Information Management* 24 (4): 283–93.

Miao, Miao, and Krishna Jayakar. 2016. "Mobile Payments in Japan, South Korea and China: Cross-Border Convergence or Divergence of Business Models?" *Telecommunications Policy* 40 (2–3): 182–96.

Milberg, Sandra J., H. Jeff Smith, and Sandra J. Burke. 2000. "Information Privacy: Corporate Management and National Regulation." *Organization Science* 11 (1): 35–57.

Murad, Mohammad H. 2010. "A Study of Digital Signature and Its Legal Implications in Context of Bangladesh." *IIUC Studies* 6: 111–22.

OECD (Organisation for Economic Co-operation and Development). 2000. *Recommendation of the OECD Council Concerning Guidelines for Consumer Protection in the Context of Electronic Commerce*. Paris: OECD.

———. 2017. "Measuring Digital Trade: Towards a Conceptual Framework." STD/CSSP/WPTGS (2017) 3. Working Party on International Trade in Goods and Trade in Services Statistics, OECD, Paris.

Olsen, G., S. Ghee Chua, O. Gergele, and F. Bartolucci. 2015. *Lifting the Barriers to E-Commerce in ASEAN*. Chicago: AT Kearney and CIMB ASEAN Research Institute.

Pappas, Christopher W. 2002. "Comparative U.S. and EU Approaches to E-Commerce Regulation: Jurisdiction, Electronic Contracts, Electronic Signatures and Taxation." *Denver Journal of International Law and Policy* 31: 325–48.

Penbera, J. J. 1999. "E-Commerce: Economics and Regulation." *S.A.M. Advanced Management Journal* 64 (4): 39–47.

Petty, R. D. 2000. "Marketing without Consent: Consumer Choice and Costs, Privacy, and Public Policy." *Journal of Public Policy and Marketing* 19 (1): 42–53.

Primo Braga, C. A. 2005. "E-Commerce Regulation: New Game, New Rules?" *Quarterly Review of Economics and Finance* 45 (2–3): 541–58.

Rezgui, Abdelmounaam, Athman Bouguettaya, and Marwa Y. Eltoweissy. 2003. "Privacy on the Web: Facts, Challenges, and Solutions." *IEEE Security and Privacy* 1 (6): 40–49.

Rizzi, Cristiano. 2002. *E-Commerce: Its Regulatory Legal Framework and the Law Governing Electronic Transactions—The Situation in Italy*. Master of law thesis, University of Exeter, United Kingdom.

Smith, H. Jeff. 2001. "Information Privacy and Marketing: What the U.S. Should (and Shouldn't) Learn from Europe." *California Management Review* 43 (2): 8–33.

Stone, Susan, James Messent, and Dorothee Flaig. 2015. *Emerging Policy Issues: Localisation Barriers to Trade*. OECD Trade Policy Papers, No. 180. Paris: OECD Publishing.

Swedish National Board of Trade. 2012. *E-Commerce: New Opportunities, New Barriers. A Survey of E-Commerce Barriers in Countries outside the EU*. Stockholm: National Board of Trade.

UNCTAD (United Nations Conference on Trade and Development). 2013a. *Information Economy Report: The Cloud Economy and Developing Countries*. Geneva: UNCTAD.

———. 2013b. *Review of E-Commerce Regulation Harmonization in the Association of Southeast Asian Nations*. Geneva: UNCTAD.

———. 2015a. *Information Economy Report: Unlocking the Potential of E-Commerce for Developing Countries*. Geneva: UNCTAD.

———. 2015b. *Review of E-Commerce Regulation Harmonization in the Economic Community of West African Countries*. Geneva: UNCTAD.

———. 2016. *Data Protection Regulations and International Data Flows: Implications for Trade and Development*. Geneva: UNCTAD.

———. 2017a. *Nepal: Rapid eTrade Readiness Assessment*. Geneva: UNCTAD.

———. 2017b. *Cambodia: Rapid eTrade Readiness Assessment*. Geneva: UNCTAD.

USITC (U.S. International Trade Commission). 2013. *Digital Trade in the U.S. and Global Economies, Part 1*. Publication 4415, Investigation 332-531. Washington, DC: USITC.

———. 2017. *Global Digital Trade 1: Market Opportunities and Key Foreign Trade Restrictions*. Publication 4716, Investigation 332-561. Washington, DC: USITC.

USTR (Office of the U.S. Trade Representative). 2013. *National Trade Estimate Report*. Washington, DC: USTR.

———. 2016. *Special 301 Report*. Washington, DC: USTR.

West, Darrell M. 2016. "Internet Shutdowns Cost Countries $2.4 Billion Last Year." Report of the Center for Technology Innovations at Brookings, Brookings Institution, Washington, DC.

# 4 Avenues for South Asian and Global Integration

Although online transactions are "space blind" and reforms facilitating them ought to be at a global scale, there is a strong justification to emphasize the importance of e-commerce in South Asia. Given that the transactions on digital platforms are blind to distance as long as delivery can be conducted efficiently, is there an argument in favor of placing this debate at a regional level? Kathuria (2018) justifies this claim by pointing out that the region discriminates against itself—and offers regional e-commerce a valuable opportunity to play the balancing act. In addition, where distance matters, as in the provision of services where physical presence is needed (for example, transport), regional e-commerce has a natural advantage.

Given the borderless nature of online transactions, no single government can unilaterally regulate e-commerce. Thus, cooperation among nations, regions, and international organizations to harmonize the existing rules and offer clarity, certainty, and predictability in online business activity is essential, as shown in table 4.1.

## E-COMMERCE AND SEARCH COSTS: EMPOWERING CONSUMERS THROUGH PLATFORMS

India's new Consumer Protection Bill, 2019, which replaces the old Consumer Protection Act of 1986, enforces consumer protection. More specifically, the bill enforces consumer rights and provides a mechanism for redressal of complaints about defects in goods and deficiency in services. The bill applies to all goods and services, as well as to all modes of transaction, including online and teleshopping. Although the 1986 act did not feature any provision governing digital transactions, the 2019 bill clearly defines direct selling, e-commerce, and an electronic service provider, enabling the central government to prescribe rules against unfair trade practices in e-commerce and direct selling.

Many other South Asian countries appear to be lagging in consumer protection vis-à-vis other regions. According to the United Nations Conference on

**TABLE 4.1** **Unleashing the potential of e-commerce: Reforms at the national, regional, and global levels**

| | LEVEL OF AGGREGATION | | |
| --- | --- | --- | --- |
| | SCOPE FOR UNILATERAL/ NATIONAL REGULATIONS | WHAT CAN BE DONE WITHIN THE SOUTH ASIAN CONTEXT? | WHAT CAN BE DONE IN A GLOBAL CONTEXT? |
| TRANSACTION COST | (1) | (2) | (3) |
| Search | Consumer protection | Integration of regional platforms (for example, large platforms with regional focus, like ecomcompany.sa) | Integration of global platforms (for example, amazon.com) |
| Contract | Data privacy | Cross-border privacy | Harmonization with international laws |
| | Electronic signatures | Cross-border recognition of digital or e-signatures (for example, single digital market such as in the European Union) | Cross-border recognition of digital or e-signatures |
| Payment | Electronic payments | Cross-border payments (for example, Paytm expanding to South Asia) | Cross-border payments |
| | Cybersecurity | Integrated cybersecurity solutions | International cooperation |
| Delivery | E-way bill | Example: DHL, South Asia | |
| | Motor Vehicle Act; stage carriage | Establishment of South Asia Post; expanding regional Motor Vehicles Agreement to include cab aggregators | |
| Tariffs | De minimis | Open intraregional e-commerce | Open cross-border e-commerce |
| | Low-value dutiable consignments | | |
| Regulations | Consumer protection | Shared institutional heritage | |
| | Competition policy | Nondiscriminatory market access and investment policies | Nondiscriminatory market access and investment policies |

*Source:* Original analysis.

Trade and Development, Bangladesh and Sri Lanka have specific consumer protection laws in the region. However, existing consumer protection legislation does not account for the impersonal nature of online transactions. In Bangladesh, the Consumer Rights Protection Act (2009) prevents any acts against consumer rights and interests in general, but not specifically for e-commerce. Although the provisions of the act also apply to the telecommunications and e-commerce sector, these mainly deal with product safety. The obligations of economic operators, by contrast, address the production of goods and services and set out comprehensive procedures for ensuring product quality and safety and repressing fraud. Other countries in the region lack provisions regarding online consumer protection.

Some big-brand e-commerce firms in the region fill the regulatory gap by adopting their own conduct codes for ensuring consumer satisfaction. For example, Myntra, an Indian e-commerce retail platform, provides a 30-day exchange window for some of its items, such as apparel and accessories, while HomeShop18 requires notification of defects within 48 hours from the time of delivery. Giants like Flipkart and Amazon also have very consumer-friendly policies, providing conflict resolution facilities between buyer and seller and granting returns and refunds even when an agreement with the seller has not been reached. In Sri Lanka, the marketplace Daraz goes as far as pushing forward a refund-only model, knowing that many of its sellers (mostly small Sri Lankan retailers approaching the online world for the first time) would not have sufficient capacity to efficiently deal with high volumes of returns during peak sales times.

E-commerce has created strong reputational incentives for firms to improve the quality of their offerings. For example, online portals (such as Amazon, e-Bay, Flipkart, Ola, and Uber) have a robust reputational feedback mechanism, such as product rating and review systems, that allows consumers a more powerful voice in economic transactions. Likewise, many "expert" product review sites deepen the dependence of large firms on feedback mechanisms that confirm their reputation on an ongoing basis and establish trust between buyers and sellers in digital space. Consumers reviewing information modify their buying decisions accordingly, which imposes costs on those sellers that miss the benchmark. For example, to retain their reputation, some firms, such as Takas (a Sri Lankan online marketplace), run functionality checks on each mobile phone sold on their website, while India Mart, a business-to-business (B2B) platform, takes complaints about suppliers listed on their online platform very seriously, to the extent of excluding them in certain cases when they are not responsive in resolving the issue raised. In comparison, the smaller firms in Sri Lanka and Nepal do not offer an appropriate return policy, perhaps because of a lack of competition and because there is lower brand equity at stake.

The reputational mechanism of digital platforms could potentially replace the role of the regulator in protecting consumers' rights. The reputational incentives motivate firms constantly to seek ways to improve the quality of their offerings. In addition, online transactions empower consumers through other means as well. For example, monitoring mechanisms in Uber and Ola allow consumers to track their rides and share their reviews in real time with friends and family. As a result of these checks and balances, bad actors get weeded out fairly quickly through better information, reputational incentives, and aggressive community self-policing. This provides incentives to motivate online firms to protect consumers even without formal legislation.

The creation of regional online retail platforms, therefore, could present an opportunity for better integrating South Asia. To the extent that consumer protection regulation is based on inadequate information for consumers, the presence of regional and international brand-name online platforms can soften the case for government intervention. These entities could leverage the geographic and cultural proximity of the countries in the region, a potential opportunity for achieving economies of scale. At the same time, firms that are sensitive to their reputation could facilitate transactions across national borders by acting as credible guarantors of consumer rights across borders. The rationale for self-regulation and business ethics adopted by online firms at the national level would apply even more when these firms are faced with the challenge of catering to a larger pool of customers. Exposure to more customers arising from regional exposure may incentivize online firms to provide better protection of the interests of consumers, including cross-border consumers. It is possible that, as online digital platforms alleviate the need for regulation, consumer welfare may ultimately be better protected by loosening traditional regulations. Increased competition, innovation, and better information obviate the need for heavy-handed regulation.

## E-COMMERCE CONTRACTS: FACILITATING DIGITAL SIGNATURES AND PROTECTING CONSUMER DATA

Most countries in South Asia have some form of regulation governing e-transactions and e-signatures. The regulations accord legal status to all electronic records and other activities carried out by electronic means. Electronic means of communication, for example, may be used to express an acceptance of contract, which has in turn the same legal validity and enforceability as if it were paper-based. Subscribers may then authenticate electronic records by affixing their digital signature. Furthermore, the laws promote e-government services and electronic communications and transactions between public and private bodies and ensure that the general principles of e-transactions are applicable also to the public sector, e-governance, and business-to-government (B2G) applications. The various national laws all envisage the establishment of a controller to supervise the activities of the certifying authorities and specify various forms and content of digital signature certificates. The acts generally acknowledge the need for recognizing foreign certifying authorities and conforming to international standards.

In theory, in all the region's countries except Bhutan and Nepal, the e-transaction regulations conform to the principles of technological neutrality and functional equivalence. However, the application of these principles in practice is a subject for debate. India's encryption laws, for example, require firms to comply with low-standard encryption to secure digitally transmitted information and procure a license should they decide to use more sophisticated and secure cryptography. Moreover, India's Information Technology Act 2000 recognizes e-transactions but primarily covers business or commercial transactions; it has no specific provision for electronic commerce for online shopping, online banking, or money transfer activities. However, several other regulations and guidelines monitor these. For example, the Payment and Settlement Systems Act 2007, which was set up by the Reserve Bank of India, provides regulation and supervision of payment systems in India.

Although laws exist, their practical enactment is hindered by the lack of clarity and institutional gaps. For example, in Bangladesh, although the Information Communication Technology Act 2006 introduces the registration and recognition of digital signatures, there is much ambiguity in the terminology of electronic and digital signatures, and therefore, it is not clear what kind of signature the act recognizes. In other countries, such as Nepal, another major obstacle is institutional gaps; although e-transactions and digital signatures are part of the policy mandated by Nepal's government, the law has not been implemented properly so far, mostly because there seems to be no agency to authorize the acceptance of digital signatures.

Although several South Asian countries have some form of data privacy regulations, they are inadequate by international standards. For example, Bangladesh, Bhutan, India, Nepal, and Pakistan have basic framework regulations[1] defining broad principles on data privacy requirements for entities that collect, process, and store personal data. Although Sri Lanka aspires to create safe practices for data protection, the country has no special provisions to protect data privacy and does not provide adequate mechanisms to remedy any misuse of information about consumers who make online purchases. However, even existing regulations look far from complete and are often characterized by significant and substantial implementation gaps. Nepal's Right to Information

Act, for instance, has features expected from data privacy laws,[2] but the act is not applicable to the private sector. Nepalese citizens have a right of access to their personal information from a wide range of government and nongovernmental bodies, but do not enjoy the same rights in their interactions with the private sector. In Pakistan, the data protection law does not apply to certain public agencies; it regulates the processing of personal or corporate data carried out by the federal, provincial, or local government. The federal government may exempt any public or private sector entity or business from operation of the act with respect to local electronic data.

Similarly, there is not full compliance with the provisions on data in India's Information Technology Act. The Information Technology Act rules incorporate, to a limited extent, the principles of collection limitation, purpose specification, use limitation, and individual participation. The rules also mandate certain requirements for the collection of information and require that it be done only for a lawful purpose connected with the function of the organization. However, the rules apply only to corporate entities, leaving the government and government bodies outside its ambit. And the rules are restricted to "sensitive personal data," which include attributes like sexual orientation, medical records, and biometrics but are silent on the larger category of personal data (Government of India 2017).[3] Furthermore, the Cyber Appellate Tribunal, a critical resolution authority on data privacy issues, appears not to have delivered any decisions, heard any new matters, or appointed a chairperson since June 2011. On the more positive side, the newly introduced Indian Consumer Protection Bill, 2019, features the disclosure of personal information given in confidence (unless required by law or in the public interest) as an unfair trade practice sanctionable with penalties.

In July 2018, the Justice Sri Krishna Committee of Experts submitted a draft Indian Personal Data Protection Bill, 2018, for consideration to the Ministry of Electronics and Information Technology for introduction in Parliament. The bill establishes requirements for the collection and processing of personal data, with significant restrictions applying to the processing of sensitive personal data. Moreover, the bill requires organizations to appoint a data protection officer and implement information security safeguards, including encryption and safeguards against misuse, unauthorized access to, modification of, disclosure, or destruction of personal data. The bill, which also proposes amendments to the Right to Information Act and Information Technology Act, applies horizontally to the government and the private sector and has an extraterritorial application to any entities providing goods and services in India and any activity involving the profiling of persons in India.

By comparison, regulations on cross-border data flows are highly stringent. In Nepal, free access to information from public agencies is restricted to Nepalese citizens and is further limited by the provision that requesters must state a reason for their information request. According to India's Information Technology Act, a corporation can transfer sensitive personal data to firms outside India only if the same level of data protection is guaranteed as that mandated under Indian rules. Such data transfers often would occur between and among units of the same corporate enterprise that is located in different countries, which thus must comply with many different regulations and heterogeneous standards. India's draft Personal Data Protection Bill, 2018, allows cross-border data transfer through a variety of channels. Nonetheless, the bill rejects consent alone as sufficient for transfer and requires the receiving country to have a sufficiently high level of data protection in place for transfers. However, the criteria for deeming the level of protection appropriate in a foreign country are left partly unspecified, as the bill generally appeals to "applicable laws and international agreements" and the effectiveness of enforcement by "authorities with the applicable jurisdiction."[4]

Establishing a mechanism for mutually recognizing e-transactions could help enhance cross-border e-commerce. For instance, the European Commission's 2014 e-IDs regulation ensures that people and businesses can use their own national electronic identification methods (e-IDs) to access public services in other European Union (EU) countries where e-IDs are available. This helped create an internal market for e-signatures and related online services across borders, by ensuring these services work across borders and have the same legal status as traditional, paper-based processes. Such harmonization and recognition of national e-IDs also help enhance savings from e-procurement.[5] If a more ambitious goal is to homogenize national legislation and set up an effective common regulatory framework across countries in the region, an obvious first step would be to set up a system for recognizing the validity of each other's e-signatures, subject to agreed-on minimum technical standards. In practice, this would entail allowing technological neutrality for signatures coming from South Asian countries and not defining any explicit prescriptions of particular types of technology or specific public key infrastructure that would be considered valid in the issuance of digital signatures and the respective certificates.

As in the European Union, a single digital market would necessitate the harmonization of regulations governing data flows. Although such regulations are much needed for stimulating cross-border e-commerce, any new or updated legislation should be implemented with caution and not cause unreasonable costs or administrative burdens to online retailers. To keep the digital transactions competitive, legislation should also recognize the economic potential of recent technical developments in information collection and analysis—such as profiling, data-driven marketing, and the use of cookies—which stimulate business innovation and provide opportunities for online retailers to optimize personalization and tailor their businesses to new consumer demands.[6] The resulting unified framework for regional data privacy should also be set up in a way that ensures nondiscrimination of regional citizens on the basis of nationality of origin. For instance, Indian laws should afford the same level of data protection to a Sri Lankan consumer of an Indian company as to an Indian customer of the same firm.

## CONSOLIDATING E-PAYMENTS: REGULATORY INFRASTRUCTURE AND CYBERSECURITY

Payment systems consist of infrastructure providers and system operators. Payment system providers (PSPs) provide the hardware, software, and network infrastructure necessary for the operation of a payment system and use payment systems to provide various financial products and services, including money transfers and payments. The operation of the system, including the regulation of access and protocols for transactions, is the prerogative of payment system operators. However, there is much heterogeneity across countries on the function and form of PSPs and payment system operators.

Regulatory structures governing payment systems vary substantially across countries and are often cumbersome and lack clarity. In Sri Lanka, for example, a restrictive environment for online payments stifles the growth of e-commerce. In particular, somewhat dated laws have held back innovation and growth in this area (Ceylon Chamber of Commerce and EIU 2017). Despite a reasonable level of development and sophistication of the banking system, imperfect competition in the banking sector seems to be a source of inefficiencies. For example, banks do not allow online payments to be performed with a debit card and only accept credit card payments. Moreover, the infrastructure for payment services is by law required to be located within a bank, which makes it difficult for nonbank PSPs to operate in the market.

Sri Lankan laws limit the types of companies that are eligible to provide financial services on e-commerce platforms. Specifically, the Payment Cards and Mobile Payment Systems Regulations No. 1 of 2013 prohibits any entity to engage in the business of or function as a service provider except under the authority and in accordance with the terms and conditions of a license issued by the Central Bank. This has resulted in limited options for transacting online. Another issue raised by many Sri Lankan private entities is the restrictions on internationally recognized payment systems, such as PayPal—these payment systems are allowed for making, but not for receiving, international payments. Some national companies are starting to fill this gap by devising new technologies, for example PayHere, which offers an integrated payment solution that would allow vendors to accept payments through multiple channels. However, banking regulations and a stringent licensing system for PSPs are posing significant barriers to innovation. For example, there are stringent requirements on the types of institutions that are eligible for receiving such licenses[7] or an unimpaired capital of at least SL Rs 150 million—which limit the opportunities for providing online payment services to banks, telecommunication companies, or large corporates with a significant amount of capital.

PSPs in India consist of bank and nonbank players.[8] As of July 2016, the PSP segment in India had eight authorized payment banks and 44 authorized prepaid payment instruments (including mobile wallets and prepaid cards) (Watal 2016). The Reserve Bank of India has also authorized eight cross-border money transfer operators and eight white-label automated teller machine operators. However, a report by Watal (2016) on digital payments in India notes that the payments ecosystem in India is largely bank-centric, with most payment systems being operated by the Reserve Bank of India or a consortium of major banks. Moreover, only bank-led PSPs have direct access to payment systems, while nonbank PSPs can access payment systems only through a member bank. Furthermore, the report highlights how the present regulatory framework fails to classify the players participating in the payments market, which creates confusion among market participants in determining what piece of regulation applies to them.

In Bangladesh, too, the slow pace of liberalization and banking practices seem to be holding back change. For example, e-retailers are not keen on accepting even national payments through cards because of a 3–4 percent commission to banks, relative to the cash-on-delivery model. Moreover, although Bangladesh Bank has introduced the two-factor authentication system, in practice most of the banks do not allow cardholders to do Internet transactions unless they call the bank to open the Internet for a specific duration.

In Pakistan, recent reform is seeking to fill existing regulatory gaps by designing a comprehensive framework for e-commerce policy. Although the resulting legislation has not yet been finalized by the Parliament, the current draft is supposed to include specific provisions for e-transactions and e-contracts. Moreover, the reform foresees amendments in the foreign exchange regulations of the State Bank of Pakistan to facilitate cross-border electronic payments, together with the finalization of a national payment gateway for international transactions.

Conversely, the lack of a solid institutional framework weakens online transactions in Nepal. Approximately 85 percent of e-commerce users in Nepal prefer cash on delivery as their payment method. Digital payment gateways, such as eSewa and IME Pay, account for only 13 percent of the users, while debit card transactions are availed by only 2 percent of users (UNCTAD 2017b). The lack of informed regulations and policies makes e-payments an extremely difficult option. E-commerce websites usually must be based outside the country, where credit card verification services are available. However, credit card transfers and transfers from e-banking websites are accepted only from Nepalis who have an international debit or credit card, which is highly restricted. Furthermore, foreign exchange is regulated and not freely available in the country.[9] The need for PSPs to collaborate with operators (banks) creates prohibitive fees for merchants, while there have also been barriers for PayPal to enter the Nepalese market.

Although digital wallets represent efficient alternatives in Nepal, the licensing procedure is extremely costly and time consuming. Nepal Rashtra Bank, the central bank, has formalized the licensing of more financial service providers and PSPs, allowing them to offer e-payment services to the public. In August 2016, when Nepal Rashtra Bank opened the PSP licensing application system, more than 67 firms applied for the licenses, but as of June 2017, Nepal Rashtra Bank had issued licenses to only three firms: eSewa, IME Pay, and Prabhu Technology (UNCTAD 2017a). Other domestic players are finding it extremely difficult to enter the market because of strict policies on the classification as PSP or payment system operator, especially capital requirements.

Nepal has proposed a strategic plan to reform its national payments system, but the institutional arrangements are far from perfect. Although there are plans for the creation of a single, unified payment gateway, this has not yet happened, and sellers face various hurdles in processing their transactions. This situation is aggravated by the lack of a single authority dealing with e-commerce matters. The lack of clear regulations and a multiplicity of institutions involved in the regulation of e-payment-related issues are serious hindrances in this direction. The payment gateway seems to be the domain, at any given time, of the Payments Department of Nepal Rashtra Bank, the Ministry of Finance, the Ministry of Technology, the Foreign Department of Nepal Rashtra Bank, and various other groups and committees. In particular, business-related aspects of e-commerce are coordinated by other ministries; for example, industries are handled by the Ministry of Industry, trade is dealt with by the Ministry of Commerce, and technology falls under the purview of the Ministry of Science, Technology, and Environment.

Regulatory barriers on foreign capital and currency flows inhibit online payments in Nepal. For example, sellers cannot receive payments in U.S. dollars, which usually results in additional cost to the firms, as they need to maintain a subsidiary abroad to receive the payment. The repatriation of the received payments is subject to high tax. These controls hinder cross-border online exports.

Moreover, because foreign exchange is regulated and foreign currency is unavailable, Nepalese consumers cannot purchase goods online on foreign sites, as foreign sellers cannot receive payment. Therefore, Nepal only has domestic e-commerce retailers, given the curbs on cross-border transactions.

These hurdles significantly constrain formal cross-border e-commerce. Although no estimates of formal e-commerce trade between India and the rest of South Asia are available, data on cross-border movement of low-value individual shipments provide some idea. The volume of and average values for bilateral small shipments between India and Bangladesh (the largest in the region) are provided in table 4.2. Assuming that around 50 percent of all of the low-value, small shipments in table 4.2 are business-to-consumer (B2C), and the rest are B2B, the value of formal, cross-border B2C e-commerce between India and Bangladesh should be between US$4 million and US$10 million per year. Of course, this is an underestimate, because it includes only DHL shipments; it does not include shipments done through other couriers or the postal department and it does not include informal e-commerce.

Despite the weak formal e-commerce linkages between India, on the one hand, and Nepal and Bangladesh, on the other, informal, cross-border e-commerce between these countries is thriving. Such informal linkages are primarily enabled by the cross-border movement of people across these two borders, through the presence of Nepali and Bangladeshi migrant workers in India.[10] Large numbers of people also travel across borders for health care, education, tourism (including religious tourism), and business.

The cross-border movement of people allows Bangladeshis and Nepalese visiting India to order online from Indian e-commerce platforms and to carry the products back with them to their home countries. In many cases, networks of families and friends browse Indian websites and instruct a member of their social circle visiting India to make the purchase. Informal agents, such as small retail shops located close to the border (in cities like Kolkata and Malda in West Bengal) often make an online purchase on behalf of Nepalese and Bangladeshi citizens for a small fee and hold the item in their shop until the buyers pick it up.

Regulatory frameworks can facilitate a larger role for the private sector to offer innovative cross-border payment solutions for the region. Paytm, for example, is an Indian electronic payment and e-commerce online platform. The company operates an online mall, which differs from a standard online marketplace in that sellers can open their "shop" on the Paytm website rather than just posting their products online. The company also has a license as a payment bank in India and operates its own payment gateway and digital wallet. These payment systems enable users to pay for purchases on Paytm and other websites,

TABLE 4.2 **Bilateral low-value individual shipments between India and Bangladesh**

| | PARCELS PER MONTH, AVERAGE | VALUATION PER PARCEL, AVERAGE (BASED ON A SMALLER SAMPLE) |
|---|---|---|
| India-Bangladesh (Indian exports) | 6,000 | US$70 to US$200 |
| Bangladesh-India (Bangladesh exports) | 4,000 | US$60 to US$150 |

*Source:* DHL.

book airplane tickets and taxis, buy airtime for their mobile phone, and pay various utility bills. Such a simplified approach to completing transactions results in better usability and ultimately more utility for customers. Clearly, cross-border payments will need the cooperation of authorities on either side of national borders. Nonetheless, if platforms like Paytm were allowed to operate across borders, they could facilitate the process, providing an efficient solution to a complex administrative problem.

Laws pertaining to cybersecurity exist in Bangladesh, Bhutan, India, Nepal, Pakistan, and Sri Lanka.[11] These laws aim to prevent unauthorized acts with respect to information systems and to provide for related offenses as well as mechanisms for their investigation, prosecution, trial, and international cooperation. Some of the main issues in cybersecurity regulation relate to crimes against information and data systems, including the unauthorized access, transmission, copying, or interference in an information system or data; computer viruses; or otherwise tampering with computer source code. The laws most often establish the prohibition of unsolicited e-mails (spam), obscene or wrongful communication, and use of a false license or certificate. Moreover, various personal crimes via the Internet are also generally included, such as personal security and security of payment, communications with children, online harassment, and criminal defamation through any information system. Pakistan's Prevention of Electronic Crimes Act (2016) also includes cyberterrorism, glorification of terrorism-related acts, hate speech, and recruitment or funding and planning of terrorism.

Cybercrime laws feature a range of content control measures as well. For example, India's Information Technology Rules provide that the central government can direct agencies to block access to information, when necessary or expedient, in the interest of the sovereignty and integrity, defense, and security of the country, public order, and friendly relations with foreign states. Indian courts have the authority to issue orders to block or filter Internet content without central government approval. Similar provisions can be found in Bangladeshi and Nepalese regulations. Pakistan also introduced other instances of content control, such as banning online protest websites and online gambling, and the proscription of unacceptable foreign broadcasting services or prohibited films. The Pakistan Telecommunication Authority also has the power to remove or block access to information on the basis of religious considerations.

Although most countries have clear prescriptions on cybersecurity, it is not obvious that they are implemented in practice. For example, the Nepalese cybercrime laws[12] provide for a tribunal dealing with cybercrimes, but private players lament that the laws have never been fully implemented and that the tribunal has not been instituted yet. In particular, UNCTAD (2017b) emphasizes that the law is outdated with respect to the new and continuously evolving technology in this space. In addition, its impact has not been as expected because of a lack of proper monitoring and the capacity to monitor its use. As a result, cybercrimes are on the rise in Nepal, with the police reporting 39 cases in 2015, a 105 percent increase from 2014 (UNCTAD 2017b). Nonetheless, for some firms, the mere existence of regulation seems to make a difference. The Nepalese online marketplace Muncha, for instance, reported that the simple introduction of those imperfect cybercrime laws coincided with a significant decline in the instances of hacking of its website.

At a regional level, cybersecurity hinges on national cybercrime laws being properly implemented. There should be a growing awareness among countries to take the security threats arising from e-commerce seriously. Creating and protecting trust, and ensuring the safety and security of electronic transactions, is a key issue for the establishment of a functioning e-commerce framework. After strengthening national capacity, then, a regional strategy could envisage integrated cybersecurity solutions. Particular emphasis could be given to the harmonization of domestic criminal laws in terms of offenses and connected provisions in the area of cybercrime, as well as the setting up of a fast and effective system of international cooperation.

These policies would have the greatest impact if they were designed in compliance with international cybersecurity best practices. In this respect, international cooperation against crimes that by their own nature transcend national or regional borders would be most critical. The main international benchmark for cybersecurity is the Budapest Convention on Cybercrime of the Council of Europe (2001), whose main objective is to pursue a common criminal policy against cybercrime. It requires states to criminalize, in their domestic legislation, a number of malicious conducts, and to establish domestic criminal procedural law powers for the investigation and prosecution of crimes committed via the Internet and computer networks.

## DELIVERY, TARIFFS, AND REGULATIONS

South Asian countries, except India, perform poorly on the World Bank's Logistics Performance Index.[13] The average Logistics Performance Index score of South Asian countries in 2018 was a very low 2.51, compared with 3.15 for East Asia and Pacific, and 2.78 for Middle East and North Africa. Afghanistan, with a score of 2.04, reflected one of the poorest logistics performances in the world. In recent years, India has emphasized logistics among its high-priority economic reforms, and in 2017 it created a new logistics division in the Ministry of Commerce and Industry. Its Logistics Performance Index score in 2018 was 3.18, placing it among the top performers in lower-middle-income countries (World Bank 2018b). The overall state of logistics in South Asia presents a challenge for the development of e-commerce, but also presents an opportunity for rapid progress, given the logistics-related innovations that e-commerce has enabled.

Delivery and distribution channels related to e-commerce come in different business models. Cross-border e-commerce can take place through the fulfillment model or direct selling. The fulfillment model is typically used for products (and brands) that have a high and predictable volume of regular sales in a particular market. E-commerce platforms or merchants trading on them would typically ship container loads of such products using low-cost ocean freight (or, in certain cases, relatively low-cost regular air freight) and store them in warehouses after customs clearance in the receiving country. When individual orders are placed online, these orders are fulfilled by delivering to the customer from these warehouses. In many respects, then, cross-border e-commerce using the fulfillment model is indistinguishable from domestic e-commerce. Such goods are listed alongside domestically sourced products in e-commerce portals and are stored in the same warehouse. Payment is made in local currency, and the last-mile logistics between the warehouse and the consumer follow the same channels.

Direct selling is more typical for goods that have a higher value or have intermittent demand and relatively lower volumes. The markets for such products are typically far less predictable, and businesses usually do not hold stocks of such products in the consumer market. This means that these products are directly purchased from international sellers, and then each individual product purchased online is sent to the consumer using international express (courier) or postal channels of distribution.

Although express and postal shipping are substantially more expensive than general ocean or air cargo, they are essential to such individualized shipping. First, online consumers expect delivery within a certain span of time, which is difficult using ocean freight or regular air cargo. Second, freight forwarders typically work with large volumes and individual, small shipments are generally not of interest to their operations. Third, consumers expect some form of tracking of their purchases in transit, which is much easier in the courier and postal ecosystem. Finally, express and postal operations are better designed to handle door-to-door delivery.

Postal and courier shipments face impediments to e-commerce delivery in South Asia. The postal letter parcel and express mail service (the expedited mail delivery managed by postal operators) in South Asia have several operational shortcomings that make them less attractive to e-commerce players. The lack of proper postal addressing systems in South Asia has made last-mile delivery a serious challenge for e-commerce companies, thus making them more dependent on more informal delivery mechanisms between delivery facilities and consumers' homes. In the context of exports from South Asian countries, constraints include the inability of postal operators to provide at-premise pickup of outbound shipments. Exporters must travel to the nearest post office, book their shipments, and drop off their goods there. And South Asian postal operators are perceived to be less reliable in the handling and security of goods. For imports, South Asian postal operators have struggled to keep pace with rapidly increasing volumes and to manage the related customs processes. Although there have been some recent developments in India Post to enhance end-to-end tracking and tracing facilities, other South Asian postal operators have to date been slower in offering full, end-to-end track and trace options.

Customs agencies have also struggled. Customs agencies across much of Asia struggle to cope with congestion and valuation issues arising from increasing cross-border parcel flows (UNESCAP and ADB 2018).

Foreign direct investment (FDI) in logistics services is generally open in most countries in the region. FDI in various aspects of logistics can improve the efficiency of parcel delivery. In South Asia, data for India, Bangladesh, Nepal, and Sri Lanka show minimal restrictions on FDI in segments relevant to small parcel delivery. However, in freight forwarding, Sri Lanka and Bangladesh cap FDI at 40 percent (table 4.3).

South Asia faces several important challenges with international express clearances. For imports, none of the countries in the region seems to have clearly defined de minimis thresholds; Indian regulations provide for a low-value non-dutiable category, limited to gifts and samples up to a certain value (table 4.4).

A low-value, dutiable category that would benefit from simplified customs clearance is not available in several countries. The value of such an option lies in simplified and expedited clearance, even more than the low duty itself. The simplified clearance system is not operative in Bangladesh and Bhutan. Where it is operative, its thresholds vary from US$200 in Nepal to US$1,500 in India (table 4.5). Overall, the lack of a simplified option or a low-value threshold reduces the percentage of shipments that can avail simplified and expedited

**TABLE 4.3 FDI restrictions on logistics services relevant to cross-border movement of small parcels**

| | | |
|---|---|---|
| India | Domestic courier | No restrictions on FDI |
| | International courier | No restrictions on FDI |
| | Road transport | No restrictions on FDI |
| | Freight forwarding | No restrictions on FDI |
| | Taxi services | No restrictions on FDI |
| Bangladesh | Domestic courier | No restrictions on FDI |
| | International courier | No restrictions on FDI |
| | Road transport | No restrictions on FDI |
| | Freight forwarding | Restricted to FDI[a] |
| | Taxi services | No restrictions on FDI |
| Nepal | Domestic courier | No FDI allowed |
| | International courier | No restrictions on FDI |
| | Road transport | No restrictions on FDI |
| | Freight forwarding | No restrictions on FDI |
| | Taxi services | No FDI allowed |
| Sri Lanka | Domestic courier | No restrictions on FDI |
| | International courier | No restrictions on FDI |
| | Road transport | No restrictions on FDI |
| | Freight forwarding | FDI restricted to 40% |
| | Taxi services | No restrictions on FDI |

*Source:* National sources.
*Note:* Taxi services have been included as a potential source of ferrying goods under a future BBIN Motor Vehicles Agreement (but this would require clarification in local goods carriage laws). Also, cab-hailing aggregators as an e-commerce service itself represents opportunities (see chapter 5). FDI = foreign direct investment.
a. A court ruling in Bangladesh has restricted FDI in freight forwarding since July 2015 under a statutory regulatory order, customs SRO No. 206-AIN/2015/43-Customs. Under this rule, companies with full foreign ownership are not allowed to obtain a freight forwarding license. Moreover, for joint venture companies, the cap on foreign ownership has been reduced from 49 to 40 percent.

**TABLE 4.4 "De minimis" in South Asia**

| | |
|---|---|
| India | About US$150 (only for gifts and samples) |
| Bangladesh | None |
| Sri Lanka | None |
| Bhutan | About US$79 |
| Nepal | None |

*Sources:* Global Express Association 2018; national sources.

**TABLE 4.5 Low-value dutiable category thresholds in South Asia**

| | |
|---|---|
| India | US$1,500 |
| Bangladesh | None |
| Sri Lanka | US$1,000[a] |
| Bhutan | None[b] |
| Nepal | US$200 |

*Source:* National sources.
a. Although Bhutan recognizes the low-value dutiable category, it does not provide a simplified clearance procedure for it.
b. If the contents are in commercial quantity less than US$1,000, customs may request the relevant bank for transaction information.

customs clearance and pushes many small shipments into the more burdensome general cargo category of customs clearances. This prevents the faster growth of e-trade, including intraregional e-trade.

## NOTES

1. Bangladesh: Information and Communication Technology Act (2006); Bhutan: Information, Communications, and Media Act (2006); India: Information Technology Act (2000) and Information Technology Rules (Reasonable Security Practices and Procedures and Sensitive Personal Data or Information Rules), also known as the "Privacy Rules" (2011); Nepal: Right to Information Act (2007); Pakistan: Electronic Data Protection Act (2005).

2. For example, right of access; right of correction; protections against access by others; restrictions on use and disclosure by government agencies; restrictions on additional uses by third parties when they do obtain access; "openness" of government practices concerning personal data; offenses and compensation provisions for breaches; an independent authority to investigate complaints and resolve disputes; and a right of appeal to the courts.

3. A more recent source of controversy in India relates to the Aadhaar (Targeted Delivery of Financial and other Subsidies, Benefits, and Services) Act (2016), which enables the government to collect identity information from citizens including their biometrics, issue a unique identification number on the basis of such information, and provide targeted delivery of subsidies, benefits, and services to them. In 2018, India's Supreme Court delivered a far-reaching judgment on several petitions related to the growing use of Aadhar. It recognized the constitutional validity of Aadhar. It asked the government to bring in a law for data protection. It agreed that the government can mandate its use to distribute government subsidies and benefits and can be required to be linked to India's tax ID number. However, the court instructed that Aadhaar could not be required for opening bank accounts or getting mobile connections. And private companies cannot ask for Aadhaar as a condition for providing services (see Gelb, Mukherjee, and Navis 2018).

4. There are also issues related to data localization requirements. For example, the White Paper on Data Protection in India (Government of India 2017) notes how localization requirements are hurting Indian startups that could rely on the cloud to host their businesses rather than having to make an expensive capital investment in computer hardware. India's draft Personal Data Protection Bill, 2018, confirms the data localization provisions introduced by previous legislation. Globally, China and India are in favor of data localization, and several other countries—including Australia, Brazil, the Republic of Korea, the Russian Federation, and Vietnam—have introduced localization laws. Japan and the United States are opposed to localization.

5. This was achieved through the STORK project, which established a pan-European electronic-identity authentication system by piloting in eight member states and associated countries of the European Union with more than 25 cross-border e-government identity services for 18 months. Following STORK's success, the STORK 2.0 project is extending e-ID interoperability to electronic representation and electronic mandates, this time involving 57 partners from 19 European member and associated states. The project pilots the updated European e-ID interoperability platform in key areas, such as e-banking, e-health, public services for business, and e-learning and academic qualifications.

6. In particular, the European Union seeks to unify the legal status for personal data protection sought by the General Data Protection Regulation (EU) 2016/679. The entry into force of the General Data Protection Regulation in May 2018 provided the first legal reference framework for the implementation of the protection of personal data and normative compliance in the European Union. See https://ec.europa.eu/commission/sites/beta-political/files/data-protection-factsheet-sme-obligations_en.pdf.

7. These include licensed commercial banks, licensed specialized banks, finance companies, or an operator that provides cellular mobile telephone services under the authority of a license issued in terms of the Sri Lanka Telecommunications Act No. 25 of 1991.

8. The present legal framework governing payment systems in India is set forth in the Payment and Settlement Systems Act, 2007 and the corresponding Regulations and Notifications. The Board for Regulation and Supervision of Payment and Settlement

System Regulations has the power to authorize, prescribe policies, and set standards for regulating and supervising all the payment and settlement systems in the country. In addition, the Reserve Bank of India has issued several master circulars, guidelines, and notifications under the Payment and Settlement Systems Act, 2007, relating to operation of payment systems, access to payment systems, operation of prepaid payment instruments, and other PSPs.

9. See https://www.export.gov/article?id=Nepal-ecommerce.

10. Outward remittances, a good proxy for migrant workers, from India to Bangladesh and Nepal are estimated at US$4 billion and US$1 billion, respectively, representing shares of about 71 and 18 percent of total outward remittances from India (World Bank 2018a). Remittances through informal channels are estimated to be much higher, especially in the case of Nepal, where its currency is pegged to the Indian rupee.

11. Bangladesh: Information and Communication Technology Act (2006); Bhutan: Information, Communications, and Media Act (2006); India: Information Technology Act (2000) and Information Technology Rules (2011); Nepal: Electronic Transactions Act 2063 (2006); Pakistan: Prevention of Electronic Crimes Act (2016); Sri Lanka: Computer Crime Act No. 24 (2007).

12. In 2008, Nepal enacted an Electronic Transaction Act, which covers electronic transactions and cybercrimes in one regulation, thereby replacing the previous Electronic and Transaction and Digital Signature Act of 2004. The Electronic Transaction Act encompasses a wide range of legal issues, including intellectual property, privacy, freedom of expression online, and jurisdiction.

13. The Logistics Performance Index ranks countries on six dimensions of trade, including customs performance, infrastructure quality, and timeliness of shipments. The data used in the ranking come from a survey of logistics professionals, who are asked questions about the foreign countries in which they operate.

## REFERENCES

Ceylon Chamber of Commerce and EIU (Economic Intelligence Unit). 2017. "Modernising Online Payments Regulations to Support E-Commerce in Sri Lanka." *Strategic Insights*, volume 4. https://docplayer.net/30964866-Modernising-online-payments-regulations-to-support-e-commerce-in-sri-lanka.html.

Gelb, Alan, Anit Mukherjee, and Kyle Navis. 2018. "What India's Supreme Court Ruling on Aadhaar Means for the Future." Center for Global Development, Washington, DC.

Global Express Association. 2018. "Overview of De Minimis Value Regimes Open to Express Shipments." https://global-express.org/assets/files/Customs%20Committee/de-minimis/GEA%20overview%20on%20de%20minimis_28%20March%202018.pdf.

Government of India. 2017. "White Paper on Data Protection." Government of India, New Delhi.

Kathuria, Sanjay. 2018. *A Glass Half Full: The Promise of Regional Trade in South Asia.* Washington, DC: World Bank.

UNCTAD (United Nations Conference on Trade and Development). 2017a. *Nepal: Rapid eTrade Readiness Assessment.* Geneva: UNCTAD.

———. 2017b. *Cambodia: Rapid eTrade Readiness Assessment.* Geneva: UNCTAD.

UNESCAP and ADB (United Nations Economic and Social Commission for Asia and the Pacific and Asian Development Bank). 2018. *Embracing the E-Commerce Revolution in Asia and the Pacific.* Manila, Philippines: Asian Development Bank.

Watal, R. P. 2016. *Medium Term Recommendations to Strengthen Digital Payments Ecosystem.* Committee on Digital Payments, Ministry of Finance. New Delhi: Government of India.

World Bank. 2018a. "Bilateral Remittance Matrix, 2017," April version. World Bank, Washington, DC. http://pubdocs.worldbank.org/en/705611533661084197/bilateralremittancematrix2017-Apr2018.xlsx.

———. 2018b. *Connecting to Compete: Trade Logistics in the Global Economy.* Washington, DC: World Bank.

# 5 Policy Options

## REGIONAL MARKET FOR E-TRANSPORT

Transport represents a fascinating application of e-commerce in services. The regulatory landscape for transportation has significant impacts on the online mediation of transport services as a form of e-commerce and on the consumption of goods transacted online.

Transport services, especially for intra-urban mobility, have emerged as one of the global success stories of e-commerce. Uber-like transport aggregators, supported by app-based transaction management, have become commonplace in many parts of the world, and the model has now spread to other areas of transportation and distribution services, such as freight forwarding (booking containers), trucking, and shared warehousing.

The distribution and delivery of goods bought online depend crucially on transportation services. E-commerce has become one of the most intensive users of logistics and transport services, given the need to deliver millions of small packages meant for individual consumption to the doors of consumers. In effect, the private act of transportation undertaken by the consumer between the physical store and home to acquire a product has been replaced by a service provided by the seller. When moving goods, air transportation is the preferred mode for intercity and international shipments. However, every e-commerce delivery also involves extensive road transportation for the goods to reach the consumer's door. In this context, China's JD.com offers an interesting case study of an e-commerce company focusing not only on selling products but also equally on logistics—"a combination of Amazon and UPS."[1]

In South Asia, e-commerce faces challenging transport-related constraints. A critical hurdle for air cargo in general—and for small, individual shipments typical of "direct selling" e-commerce in particular—is the lack of adequate handling and processing infrastructure in smaller regional airports. This issue is acute in a vast country such as India. More than 90 percent of the country's air cargo shipments are handled in six main airports (Delhi, Mumbai, Bengaluru, Chennai, Kolkata, and Hyderabad), which poses significant challenges for large parts of the country located at some distance from a major air hub. Large parts of north, central, northeastern, and southeastern India, like the more remote parts of Odisha and Andhra Pradesh, are more than 400 kilometers from a major airport with adequate processing and handling infrastructure.

Bangladesh and Nepal are even more constrained by the lack of air cargo infrastructure and connectivity. Large parts of Bangladesh that are not in the proximity of Dhaka or Chittagong are difficult to serve logistically for any air cargo solution, especially given the country's relatively poor road infrastructure. Nepal's mountainous terrain makes for severe logistical impediments to any road-based solution, while Kathmandu remains the sole major air hub with any capability to process cargo.

In some cases, parts of Nepal and Bangladesh could potentially be served by Indian airports. For example, parts of western Bangladesh are close to Kolkata, and certain areas of Nepal could be accessible from Varanasi, which is emerging as a fast-growing regional airport with international air connections. However, regulatory restrictions related to customs and transport laws prevent effective cross-border trucking that would allow these parts of Bangladesh or Nepal to use Indian airports (or vice versa).

The acute lack of logistics integration in the South Asian region is often countered by the sustained flows of informal cross-border e-commerce. This informal model could well become a robust and regular channel of trade if cheap transport options and customs-related facilitation were available for low-value products crossing regional borders.

Developing such an integrated model in South Asia would require the countries to allow each other's vehicles into their territories. Except for traffic between India and Nepal, at present trucks cannot cross borders; goods must be transloaded at the border, often manually (given the lack of mechanization and development of modern automated truck bays at customs stations). The costs and delays associated with this process are significant. Moreover, in addition to trucks not being able to cross borders, South Asian countries do not allow semi-trailers and trailers to cross borders, in contrast to what happens in other parts of the world, such as Europe, large parts of the Middle East, North and East Africa, and North America.

The Bangladesh, Bhutan, India, Nepal Motor Vehicles Agreement (BBIN MVA), originally signed in 2015, provides a promising framework for addressing this issue. The agreement allows vehicles from member states to enter each other's territory for the transportation of cargo and passengers. It also abolishes cross-border transloading of goods for cargo vehicles, which would be tracked electronically and receive the relevant permits online. Bhutan subsequently indicated that it would prefer to wait, so the agreement has effectively become the Bangladesh, India, and Nepal (BIN) MVA.

Despite the good starting point offered by BIN MVA, some details need to be addressed to ensure maximum effectiveness of the agreement. In particular, the agreement needs to address several critical areas related to the management of cross-border transport and associated customs clearance procedures (Banerjee 2016).

For example, trucks, trailers, and semitrailers should be allowed to cross borders with minimum restrictions, through simplifying customs and clearance procedures that have typically led to border congestion. Off-border clearances could instead be put in place, allowing customs and other processes to take place at notified customs points inside the country, closer to where the consignor and consignee are located. Using GPS technology and passive radio-frequency identification technology seals, customs at the border can ensure that the goods in a vehicle have not been tampered with after having been checked and sealed by customs inside the country.

Furthermore, customs rules should be made flexible enough to allow even small traders and small and medium-size enterprises (SMEs) to benefit from the MVA. This would mean allowing multiconsignment goods (that is, several different shipments for different commercially registered entities) to be carried in the same truck or conveyance, allowing the development of freight networks and the less-than-a-truckload services typically preferred by SMEs. Moreover, SMEs would benefit if the clearance of low-value, small shipments was allowed at land customs stations. India is the only country that has a provision along these lines in its customs rules, but limits it to just two locations on the India-Bangladesh border. A more effective approach would be to allow inland clearances of low-value, small shipments, including for shipments where the recipient is an individual and not a registered legal entity.

South Asia could envision significant developments in digitally enabled mobility. In particular, an emerging trend is to use app-based aggregator models in goods transport, expanding shared mobility to hybrid models of "goods and passengers" transport. An example of this is the extension of the Uber model to goods transport, which entails linking individual truckers and trucking companies to consumers through apps that also manage bookings, payments, and other value-added services, such as insurance and commercial and legal document preparation for carriage. Uber has launched Uber Freight,[2] while another international example is Saloodo, an initiative of Deutsche Post DHL Group.[3]

Passenger mobility can also be leveraged to enhance cargo solutions. For example, small consignments can easily travel from urban distribution hubs to consumer centers in smaller towns and villages using the dense network of passenger buses that crisscross most parts of South Asia. An extension of app-based e-commerce mediation could manage payment, pick up, and delivery online, facilitating many "last-mile" delivery hurdles and at the same time helping reduce road congestion and traffic.

Similarly, intracity distribution of goods could gain from hybrid goods-passenger combinations if app-based aggregators were also allowed to carry cargo in the boot of their passenger vehicles. With this model, it is possible that roughly 30,000 taxis with their boot space could replace between 1,000 and 1,500 trucks on the road (depending, among other things, on how many trips a car does compared with a truck), reducing traffic and pollution and bringing down the cost of urban distribution of goods.

The rollout of such hybrid services is prevented by the regulations currently contained in the motor vehicle acts of South Asian countries. For example, the commercial transport of passengers in India is regulated by the Motor Vehicles Act, 1988. The act recognizes three distinct types of passenger transport (contract carriage, stage carriage, and tourist vehicle), but these definitions in practice impose many regulatory inflexibilities that prevent the development of new models of passenger transportation empowered by information technology (IT) and digitization. For example, contract carriage essentially defines the ecosystem of traditional taxi services and, as per the interpretation of the law, a vehicle that is registered to provide a contract carriage service cannot pick up or drop off passengers during a journey. Tourist vehicles are a special category of contract carriage, being licensed taxis that can operate across state borders, and as such, they also are not allowed to pick up or drop off passengers along their journey. The right to pick up and drop off passengers is instead reserved for vehicles registered as stage carriage, which defines the ecosystem for traditional bus or shared mobility services.

Because the Indian law requires a vehicle to be registered as contract carriage or stage carriage, but not both, these definitions do not allow the growth of hybrid passenger transport that would enable a vehicle to switch between point-to-point exclusive passenger mobility and longer-route shared mobility by picking up and dropping off passengers along the way. However, the new ecosystem of personal mobility based on e-commerce could easily manage and provide such flexible, hybrid models of mobility, in turn optimizing vehicle use and route viability.

Another major restriction in the Indian law on commercial passenger transport is that stage carriage vehicles need to carry more than six passengers. This means that smaller cars, which form the backbone of intracity taxi services, cannot qualify for shared mobility licenses. Although the regulation originated from legitimate concerns about passenger safety and passenger rights, the ground reality in South Asian cities today has evolved, and such regulatory restrictions have come to represent a source of unintended inefficiency. As Kumar et al. (2016) point out, informal public transport in India already sees many vehicles plying passengers without requisite permits, providing contract carriage or stage carriage services in hybrid models, and various forms of shared mobility. For instance, it is not infrequent for school buses and private cars to offer point-to-point or shared riding services when they are not engaged in their primary activity.

India's Motor Vehicles Act requires any given legal person to be the owner of a vehicle or act as an agent for the owner. As this provision does not account for vehicle aggregators, such as those that provide app-based shared mobility services like Uber, changes to the regulatory framework are being contemplated to include the category of aggregator as an entity that "owns and manages a web-based software application, and by means of the application and communication device, enables a potential customer to connect with persons providing a particular service under the brand name or trade name of the aggregator."

Another problematic definition in India's Motor Vehicles Act 1988 is that of goods transport vehicles, which the law identifies as those that are adapted and constructed to carry goods. Importantly, goods refer to all materials carried by a vehicle other than living human persons, which means that vehicles registered as goods transport vehicles cannot carry passengers. Thus, the dual use of a vehicle for the transport of goods and passengers, such as taxis carrying goods in the car boot, is legally not allowed. Although app-based truck aggregators have been managing to operate as "agents," as defined by the Motor Vehicles Act, and many passenger vehicles informally carry goods and vice versa, the hybrid model is formally absent in the Indian regulation.

Furthermore, India's Carriage by Road Act, 2007, requires providers of regular cargo carriage services to have at least two commercial vehicles registered under their name and to have a net worth of at least INR 500,000 (US$7,000). Because most vehicle owners operating through app-based aggregator services own just one vehicle and often cannot count on significant net capital worth, this provision represents another stumbling block for the development of a modern transport framework that takes full advantage of the opportunities offered by digital solutions.

FIGURE 5.1
**Regional market for e-transport**

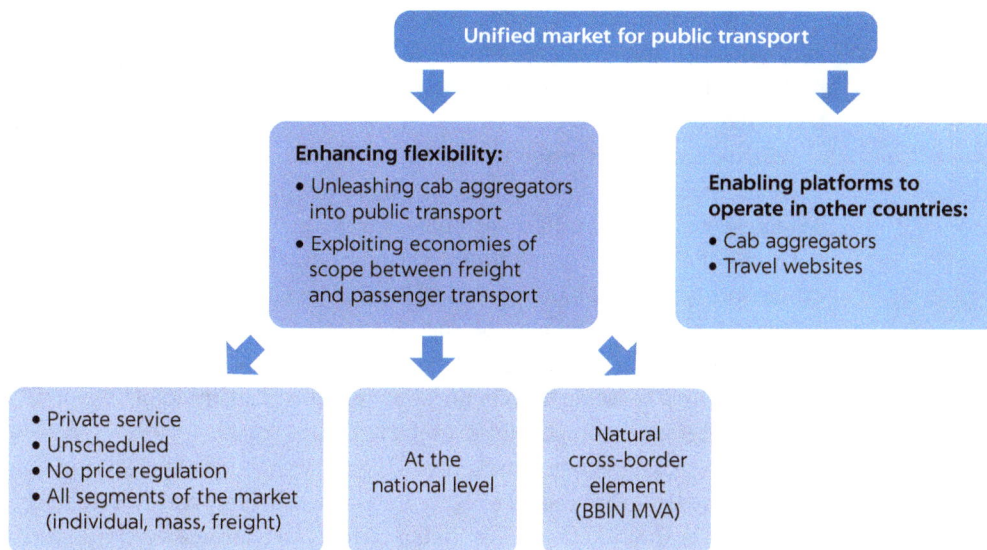

Unified market for public transport

**Enhancing flexibility:**
- Unleashing cab aggregators into public transport
- Exploiting economies of scope between freight and passenger transport

**Enabling platforms to operate in other countries:**
- Cab aggregators
- Travel websites

- Private service
- Unscheduled
- No price regulation
- All segments of the market (individual, mass, freight)

At the national level

Natural cross-border element (BBIN MVA)

*Source:* Original analysis.
*Note:* BBIN MVA = Bangladesh, Bhutan, India, Nepal Motor Vehicles Agreement.

In sum, there is a distinct case for substantially reforming the domestic laws and regulations of South Asian countries, to formalize the existing broad range of e-commerce-based transport services. This would first and foremost establish clear rules of the game and grant adequate legal protection to service providers, operators, and consumers in national arenas. Once this is done, a promising next step would be to gradually facilitate the cross-border market for such services in South Asia, for example, starting from the Bangladesh, India, and Nepal cluster, and capitalizing on the formal and informal links that already exist within the region. Historically, the transport hubs within the BBIN subregion have always seen thriving cross-border transit of goods and passengers, especially between India and Bangladesh and between India and Nepal, and they are increasingly witnessing growing exchanges between Nepal, Bhutan, and Bangladesh. The BIN Motor Vehicles Agreement is expected to strengthen these ties, especially if certain crucial refinements of customs and clearance rules are introduced in the agreement. For app-based, shared mobility solutions, once the various national regulations are updated to account for the de facto existence of hybrid models of commercial carriage of goods and passengers, the cross-border supply of these services could represent a further driver of increased efficiency, reduced road and customs congestion, and deeper regional integration (see figure 5.1).

## UNIFIED MARKET FOR B2C E-COMMERCE

Similar to the European Union's Digital Single Market proposal, South Asia could aspire to have a regionally integrated business-to-consumer (B2C) e-commerce market. Although a digital single market is not yet a reality in the European Union, a sustained effort toward this goal will enable people and businesses to trade with fewer barriers. For now, online marketplaces in Europe are mainly domestic, with only 7 percent of SMEs selling cross-border. It has been estimated that the digital single market could contribute €415 billion to the European economy, boosting jobs, growth, competition, investment, and innovation (European Commission 2015). Figure 5.2 illustrates how a unified market could be designed to overcome transaction costs and ensure the protection of the South Asian consumer.

A digital South Asian market will require tariff reforms and harmonization of national regulations pertaining to e-commerce. The main regulatory effort will be represented by tariff reforms and the reconciliation of national regulations in the areas of electronic transactions, data privacy, consumer protection, and cybersecurity. The Digital Single Market strategy launched by the European Commission in 2015, as well as the electronic commerce chapter in the Comprehensive and Progressive Agreement for Trans-Pacific Partnership (CPTPP) among 11 Pacific Rim countries, are prominent international examples, and are addressed in this chapter as useful reference points.

The success of integrated markets will require protection of the South Asian consumer by way of appropriate regulations on data privacy and cybersecurity. These efforts should create a unified and integrated framework to ensure effectiveness through cooperation across national authorities. The key principles sustaining this framework should be harmonization, waiver of intraregional data localization requirements, and nondiscrimination. Specifically, (a) cybersecurity laws and data privacy laws should be harmonized among countries in the region, and opportunities for cooperating on major cybercrime issues should be pursued by national authorities; (b) data should be allowed to

FIGURE 5.2

**Unified market for B2C e-commerce in South Asia**

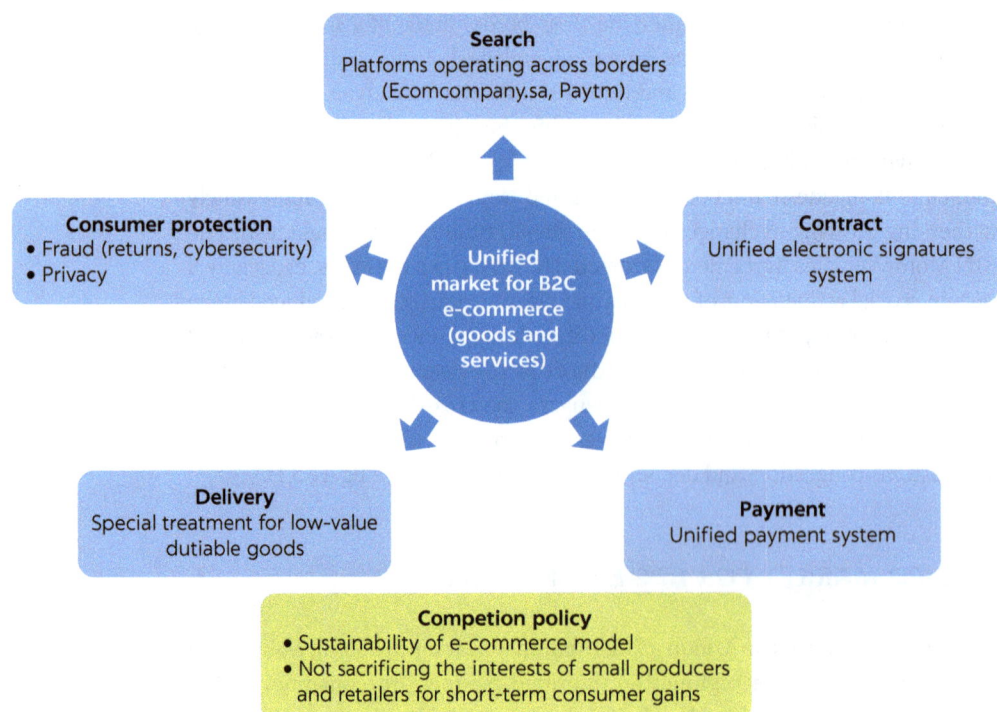

Source: Original analysis.
Note: B2C = business-to-consumer.

move freely within the region in the same way as they would within the national borders of each participant country, and companies operating in one South Asian country should not be required to set up data-processing and storage facilities in other countries in the region to be allowed to operate there; and (c) the same level of protection should be granted and enforced for the personal data, sensitive information, and cybersecurity of all South Asian consumers, regardless of their country of origin.

The e-commerce chapter of the CPTPP Agreement mandates that each country must adopt or maintain consumer protection laws to proscribe fraudulent and deceptive commercial activities that are harmful to consumers engaged in online commercial activities (Article 14.7). The agreement stresses the importance of cooperation between the countries' respective national consumer protection agencies or other relevant bodies regarding activities related to cross-border e-commerce. Article 14.11 also mandates partner countries to allow the cross-border transfer of data, including personal information. Specifically, national laws are allowed to restrict cross-border transfers only if they (a) are necessary "to achieve a legitimate public policy objective"; (b) are not applied "in a manner which would constitute a means of arbitrary or unjustifiable discrimination"; (c) are not a "disguised restriction on trade"; and (d) do not impose "restrictions on transfers of information greater than are required to achieve the objective."

In the European Digital Single Market, European Union–wide enforcement of consumer rights works through a strong cooperation effort among national public authorities.[4] A key piece of legislation to boost fairness in e-commerce transactions is the Unfair Commercial Practices Directive,[5] which has been complemented by a guidance note on its application to the online sector. In 2016, the European Commission proposed a reform of the Consumer Protection Cooperation Regulation[6] to ensure a more efficient cooperation framework among national authorities in fostering enforcement and stopping online infringements. The regulation aims to provide a single procedure, launched and coordinated by the European Commission, for European Union–wide problems. The European Union–wide online dispute resolution platform helps consumers and traders solve disputes over online transactions (within and cross-border), without going to court.

For cybersecurity, member states and European Union institutions abide by the European Cybersecurity Strategy (2013). The essential legislative component of this strategy is the 2016 Directive on Security of Network and Information Systems.[7] The European Commission's Communication on "Strengthening Europe's Cyber Resilience System and Fostering a Competitive and Innovative Cybersecurity Industry" (2016)[8] calls for the improvement of member states' coordination mechanisms to prepare for large-scale cyber incidents and outlines measures to strengthen the European single market for cybersecurity products and services. Among the key initiatives under the communication, a contractual public-private partnership was signed between the European Commission and the European Cyber Security Organisation[9] to invest jointly in cybersecurity research and innovation.

The European Union's Digital Single Market proposal provides guidance on rules for harmonization of data protection regulations. The General Data Protection Regulation[10] covers the processing of personal data, with special rules for the electronic communications sector laid out in the ePrivacy Directive (2002).[11] To preserve the efficacy of the ePrivacy rules in light of technological innovation, the European Commission's proposal for an ePrivacy Regulation (2017)[12] complements and particularizes the General Data Protection Regulation for the protection of personal data and respect for private life. The regulation protects the confidentiality of electronic communications (content and metadata), mandating that electronic communications service providers process electronic communications data without the users' consent only for specific purposes, such as technical storage for transmission, billing, or ensuring the quality of the service. The new ePrivacy proposal is technology-neutral and will apply to traditional telecom operators and "over-the-top" service providers (for example, Skype and WhatsApp). For online tracking, to minimize the number of cookie banners on websites, users are required to choose a specific privacy setting when they install their browser, which they can easily modify at any point in time.

Under certain situations, the private sector could take the lead in building viable practices that it is already implementing in the market. For instance, it is quite likely that the spread of reputable e-commerce platforms beyond their respective domestic borders and into the regional space could prove a very effective tool for better consumer protection, reducing fraud, and ensuring good data privacy standards, arising from the self-regulation adopted by large firms to safeguard their reputation and increase customer loyalty. Search costs would be minimized by allowing e-commerce platforms to operate cross-border, rather than requiring them to establish their presence in several segmented national markets. This would open the possibility of exploiting economies of scale and reaching a larger pool of customers. For consumers, the move would lead to greater choice, lower costs, and access to the consumer protection best practices that big companies adopt for quality control, refunds, and return policies.

Complementary regulations can facilitate the interoperability of regional digital platforms. In its Communication on Online Platforms and the Digital Single Market Opportunities and Challenges for Europe (2016), the European Commission outlined the key issues identified in the assessment of online platforms. In this communication, it set out its position on the innovation opportunities and regulatory challenges presented by online platforms and committed to promoting further interoperability actions through issuing principles and guidance on electronic identification interoperability. Other regulations of the European Union (like the updated Guidance on the Unfair Commercial Practices Directive) are also relevant to online platforms, including professional diligence duties, transparency obligations, and competition policy.

The establishment of consumer trust would need to go hand in hand with the establishment of a unified regime for e-signatures and e-transactions. If every country sets different standards for what can be considered a valid proof of transaction and a binding expression of consent, then any exchange involving parties located in different countries potentially could be subject to litigation and dispute. The resulting legal uncertainty and fragmented business environment will eventually harm consumers through less competitive offers and limited choice. For electronic transactions, Article 14.5 of the CPTPP requires governments to maintain frameworks that are consistent with the United Nations Commission on International Trade Law Model Law on Electronic Commerce 1996 or the United Nations Convention on the Use of Electronic Communications in International Contracts. Similarly, the European Union has put forward two proposals for directives on certain aspects of B2C contracts that advocate for the full harmonization of key contract rules on, respectively, online and other distance sales of goods,[13] and the supply of digital content.[14] Articles 14.5 and 14.6 of the CPTPP also clearly define digital signatures; therefore, the legal validity of a signature cannot be denied purely on the grounds that it is in electronic form.[15]

Integrating South Asian digital markets will need a unified payments system. Such a payments mechanism would eliminate the impediments encountered today by so many citizens in the region when trying to purchase or sell internationally. The policy restrictions on using national credit or debit cards for cross-border purchases, accepting dollar payments, and allowing internationally recognized payment providers (such as PayPal) to access certain national markets are seriously hampering the development of the e-commerce sector in many countries. Any attempt at regional e-commerce integration will need to address this fundamental issue. Cash on delivery for international purchases could be an easy first step in this direction, but trust, which is already a significant issue in e-commerce, is likely to play an even bigger role cross-country, therefore stifling international transactions. Digital wallets and mobile money are becoming ever more popular payment methods with consumers and vendors for their immediacy and ease of use; therefore, it could be worth exploring these possibilities. Digital platforms that rely on their own payment systems could also have a substantial facilitating role, if they could operate cross-border.

Establishing a unified payments system requires a multilateral regulatory effort. For example, the Second Payment Services Directive is a fundamental piece of payment legislation in Europe that became effective across member states in January 2018. It sets out a common legal framework for businesses and consumers when making and receiving payments within the European Economic Area. The directive relies on a commitment to increase competition in the payment system, as well as to make Internet and mobile payments easier and to allow customers to manage their accounts more efficiently. For example, the Second Payment Services Directive introduces two new legal categories of third-party payment providers[16] and allows third-party providers of financial services to operate in the entire European Union as long as they are licensed by their domestic financial authorities.

To address delivery costs, the region needs to harmonize regulations pertaining to international e-commerce of small, low-value dutiable consignments. In 2012, cross-border delivery was considered to be an obstacle by 57 percent of retailers in Europe (*Eurobarometer* 2015), while nearly 50 percent of online consumers worried about the delivery in cross-border transactions (European Commission 2012). In particular, high delivery charges for cross-border parcel services prevent small retailers from selling or buying more, even across the European Union. The European Union's Digital Single Market strategy makes a proposal on parcel delivery,[17] which seeks to increase price transparency and regulatory oversight of cross-border parcel delivery services. The regulation proposes to equip national postal regulators with much-needed data for monitoring cross-border markets and checking the affordability of prices. It will also encourage competition by requiring transparent and nondiscriminatory third-party access to certain cross-border parcel delivery services and infrastructure. The European Commission proposes to publish the public list prices of universal service providers to increase peer competition and tariff transparency. Moreover, the regulation requires universal service providers to offer access to their cross-border networks to new market entrants, to give customers a greater choice of cross-border parcel services.

South Asia could learn from the several approaches followed by the European Union to address the challenges facing cross-border parcel delivery. For example, the European Commission published a consultation to seek the views of all interested parties on possible areas for improvement that could enhance the cross-border parcel delivery market within the European Union. In another instance, the European Commission set up a LinkedIn group with agents interested in the challenges pertaining to parcel delivery. This group allows participants to share practical concerns when shipping across borders, learn about solutions that others are developing, and contribute ideas to help achieve a better "single market for parcel delivery." These consultations and group discussions revealed that the inadequacy of cross-border delivery featured as the most prominent obstacle for online retailers and consumers, hindering their deeper participation in cross-border e-commerce. The differences in technical methods at the European Union level within the universal postal service (in particular for external measurement of the quality of service performance) and lack of the interoperability of postal industry stakeholders could be critical in ensuring a seamless parcel delivery method across the region.

Clearance of packages valued above the de minimis value and up to a threshold limit should be simplified. In practice, this means adopting a different and predictable approach for goods up to a threshold limit, for instance, through an easier system for goods declaration, or by providing information that enables simple quantification and payment of payable duties and taxes. In this context, diverse requirements across countries generate costs and uncertainties, hampering compliance and discouraging e-commerce (World Customs Organization 2015). Harmonized regional solutions would at the same time restore appropriate incentives for e-commerce and facilitate revenue collection by governments. The exchange of information between customs authorities and e-commerce intermediaries should be promoted, as well as strengthened administrative cooperation and exchange of information between the authorities of importing and exporting countries.

## NOTES

1. Quote from Barboza (2015) in the *New York Times*. The article highlights how JD.com has increasingly moved to developing its logistics capabilities in the battle for market share in the world's second-largest economy. At the time of writing of the article, JD.com's distribution network included 15 logistics parks, more than 500 warehouses, nearly 7,000 delivery and pickup stations, and a quarter-million transportation and delivery vehicles, including some operated by partners.
2. See https://freight.uber.com/.
3. See https://www.saloodo.com/en.
4. The European Union adopted the Digital Single Market strategy in May 2015. It comprises 16 specific initiatives and had delivered the main legislative proposals as of its mid-term review in 2017. These pertain to e-commerce, copyright, audiovisual and media services, telecoms review, ePrivacy, harmonization of digital rights, affordable parcel delivery, and harmonized value-added tax rules.
5. Directive 2005/29/EC.
6. COM (2016) 283 final.
7. Directive (EU) 2016/1148 of the European Parliament and of the Council of July 6, 2016, concerning measures for a high common level of security of network and information systems across the European Union.
8. COM (2016) 410 final.

9. The European Cyber Security Organisation gathers more than 180 companies, associations, and public and regional authorities with a stake in cybersecurity.

10. Regulation (EU) 2016/679 of the European Parliament and of the Council of April 27, 2016, on the protection of natural persons with regard to the processing of personal data and the free movement of such data and repealing Directive 95/46/EC (General Data Protection Regulation).

11. Directive 2002/58/EC of the European Parliament and of the Council of July 12, 2002, concerning the processing of personal data and the protection of privacy in the electronic communications sector.

12. COM (2017) 10.

13. COM (2015) 635 final.

14. COM (2015) 634 final.

15. However, Article 14.6 allows parties to establish performance standards for authentication and requirement for certification by an accredited authority. These performance and certification measures can operate even if they prevent parties from determining their own authentication method or proving legal compliance to a judicial or administrative body.

16. Specifically, the new entities are account information service providers, which act as aggregators of data relating to customers' accounts held across different payment institutions into one overview; and payment initiation service providers (PISPs), which establish a software bridge between the website of the merchant and the online banking platform of the payer's bank to initiate payment on behalf of the payer. The PISP solution involves fewer parties and does not require the customer to reveal payment card details; an example is peer-to-peer transfers between friends (EVRY 2017).

17. COM (2016) 285.

## REFERENCES

Banerjee, Pritam. 2016. "Operationalizing Connectivity and Trade Facilitation: Role of BBIN Motor Vehicles Agreement." *Asian Journal of Transport and Infrastructure* 19 (2): 72–89.

Barboza, David. 2015. "China's Other E-Commerce Giant Follows Its Own Path." *New York Times*, January 26.

*Eurobarometer*. 2015. "Business Attitude towards Cross-Border Sales and Consumer Protection." Analytical report, *Flash Eurobarometer* 224.

European Commission. 2012. "An Integrated Parcel Delivery Market for the Growth of E-Commerce in the EU." Green Paper 29.11.2012 COM (2012) 698, European Commission, Brussels. http://ec.europa.eu/internal_market/consultations/docs/2012/parcel-delivery/121129_green-paper-parcel-delivery_en.pdf.

———. 2015. "A Digital Single Market Strategy for Europe: Analysis and Evidence." Commission staff working document SWD (2015) 100, European Commission, Brussels. https://ec.europa.eu/digital-single-market/en/news/digital-single-market-strategy-europe-analysis-and-evidence-swd2015-100-final.

———. 2016. "Questions and Answers: Boosting E-Commerce in the EU." Communication IP/16/1887, Press Release Database, European Commission, Brussels, May 25.

EVRY. 2017. "PSD2: Strategic Opportunities beyond Compliance." White paper, EVRY, Oslo.

Kumar, Megha, Seema Singh, Akshima T. Ghate, Sarbojit Pal, and Sangeetha A. Wilson. 2016. "Informal Public Transport Modes in India: A Case Study of Five City Regions." *International Association of Traffic and Safety Sciences Research* 39: 102–09.

World Customs Organization. 2015. "E-Commerce and Revenue Collection." *WCO News* 78: 38–43.

# 6 Conclusions
## A PRACTICAL APPROACH TO ENHANCING E-COMMERCE WITHIN SOUTH ASIA

This policy note analyzes the key drivers of e-commerce, using a conceptual framework that emphasizes the role of e-commerce in reducing policy and nonpolicy transaction costs. It includes the results of a survey of 1,688 merchants and 539 e-commerce firms in seven South Asian countries, as well as a qualitative analysis of meetings with firms operating in this space in three South Asian countries: India, Nepal, and Sri Lanka. According to the survey, less than 40 percent of the firms reported online activity in buying and selling goods and services. Small exporting firms in South Asia were more likely to have online activity, compared with small firms that did not export. Much of the international trade in South Asia was reported to be with extraregional trade partners, such as China, the United Kingdom, and the United States. Although there were country variations in reported obstacles to cross-border e-commerce, among the top challenges faced by firms in the region were the high cost of cross-border logistics, onerous customs regulations (like obtaining clearance for low-value shipments), and high taxes alongside other trade barriers in the export markets.

In principle, specific policies can affect e-commerce within the country or region or with the rest of the world. In practice, there are overlaps as well as differences between the policies along these three dimensions. For example, if Sri Lanka mandates a consumer protection policy for its territory, all firms delivering to Sri Lankan consumers—whether based in Sri Lanka, South Asia, or outside South Asia—would need to adhere to the policy. In addition, national policies that deepen the adoption of e-commerce will affect all players. However, policies could also favor regional players, which would be the e-commerce equivalent of regional preferential arrangements. This concluding chapter focuses on the regional aspect, while recognizing that many e-commerce policies will and ideally should affect all firms, irrespective of location or origin.

There is growing evidence of the potential for e-commerce within South Asia, on the basis of current transactions, formal and informal, as well as the increasing role of e-commerce in mediating traditional trade (starting with the search element). This evidence includes informal business-to-consumer (B2C) trade; medical services facilitated by e-commerce; potential trade in digital products such as movies, music, and education services; and potential trade in high-demand products such as Bangladeshi Jamdani sarees, Indian sarees, women's undergarments made in Sri Lanka, women's suits and cotton wear made in Pakistan, and so forth.

The sequence of the development of regional e-commerce could be thought of as a three-stage development. The first stage is the existing informal e-commerce, which mediates the tariff and logistics challenges. The second stage would be the simplification of tariffs, payments, and logistical barriers, and consumers depending on the reputation of big firms as a substitute for formal, robust contractual and consumer protection mechanisms. The third stage would be more formalized regional platforms and regulations, which governments are more likely to be interested in if the second stage reaches a critical mass.

What kind of policy framework will help to catalyze e-commerce within South Asia? The previous chapters have laid out the core issues and drawn on global experience in cross-border e-commerce, especially from the European Union and the 11 countries that are part of the Comprehensive and Progressive Agreement for Trans-Pacific Partnership (CPTPP). This chapter focuses largely on second-stage issues; that is, it adopts a practical approach to regional e-commerce with large-platform firms, enabling e-commerce transactions on the strength of their reputation. These could then be followed by the more advanced proposals of stage three that consider regulatory harmonization in several spheres, as in the case of the European Union. All the ideas suggested here address policy frictions relating to core constraints that affect cross-border e-commerce, namely, contract recognition, payments, consumer protection, logistics, and tariffs.

## ENABLING REGIONAL CONTRACTING

Cross-border e-commerce could take place under different formal arrangements. Today, some e-commerce platforms in India are already selling across borders informally. One way this arrangement could be formalized would be to allow companies to establish a regional platform, for which the suffix could be ".sa." Such a platform may initially limit the range of products listed to those with lower tariffs and costs of delivery. Alternatively, companies could supply cross-border through their national platforms, with cross-border recognition of digital contracts. From a regional perspective, the ".sa" model is more attractive because it could enable the development of regional guidelines for the operation of e-commerce platforms and allow an expanding set of countries to sign on to initial guidelines negotiated between, say, two countries. The national platform model, by contrast, would require a series of bilateral negotiations and guidelines, which could make it more difficult to aggregate later into a regional solution.[1]

In either case, countries would need to agree to recognize each other's digital transaction mechanisms to make the cross-border contracts legally binding. To the extent that national approaches are broadly in line with the United Nations Commission on International Trade Law Model Law on Electronic Commerce, or the United Nations Convention on the Use of Electronic Communications in International Contracts, the recognition of digital transactions can be facilitated. However, there is still a lack of clarity, and there are institutional gaps in the legal frameworks for e-transactions within South Asian countries that would need to be remedied (see chapter 5). Countries would also need to cooperate on data privacy laws and cybersecurity to protect consumer data irrespective of consumers' country of origin and to pursue cybercrime issues at a regional level.

## FACILITATING PRACTICAL PAYMENT SOLUTIONS

A fundamental issue is consumer access to foreign exchange. For example, national credit or debit cards cannot be used for cross-border payments in Nepal, and PayPal cannot be used to receive payments from overseas in Bhutan, Nepal, and Sri Lanka. Practical fixes have already emerged in the private sector; for example, Nepalese are ordering on India-based websites such as Flipkart and Amazon.in and having the products delivered to them through friends and relatives who travel or work in India. Another option is cash on delivery, but that solution would have to contend with trust issues and the conversion of local currency to international currency, unless, for example, platform firms like Flipkart invest and incorporate in Nepal.

More efficient solutions would allow payment initiation service providers[2] (PISPs), which provide a software bridge between banks and merchants, to receive money in each country for goods and services exported. For imports, central banks could, if they wished, cap the amount of cross-border purchases per year per consumer via e-commerce, which can also be done through PISPs (to make things easier for consumers). To facilitate regional transactions, perhaps 50 percent of this cap could be restricted to purchases from within South Asia. Depending on their comfort levels, central banks could increase these caps over time.

These would be interim solutions until the regulations enable cross-border PISPs to operate throughout South Asia (or even in subregions). An option would be a South Asia digital wallet, which is also an efficient payments solution. For example, in India, Paytm, Flipkart, and Amazon.in now provide their own digital wallets. Access to these services from other South Asian countries would require regulatory permission from the respective country authorities and compliance from the merchants.

## PROTECTING THE CONSUMER

Regulations on consumer protection are uneven in South Asia. While policy plays catchup, it is possible that firms can fill the void. Success in e-commerce depends critically on consumer confidence in the firm's ability to deliver the promised product and quality and to ensure a simple return policy. The instantaneous ratings that consumers provide prompt e-commerce firms to constantly improve the quality of their offerings, which they do by penalizing erring suppliers and implementing a consumer-oriented return or redressal policy. Strong competition among existing and new e-commerce firms further propels this logic.

Consumers in countries such as India and Sri Lanka tend to rely on the reputation of large digital platforms—which often go beyond the letter of the law—to protect their interests. This same reputation effect is likely to prevail across borders and protect consumer interests in countries receiving products from firms in neighboring markets. The one issue here can be cross-border product returns, which may be too cumbersome from a regulatory standpoint. To get around this, firms may prefer to provide a return solution within the consumer's country, which would require cross-border investment or tie up with a local firm. This may possibly imply an initial limited menu of product offerings, which could gradually increase as confidence increases on all sides: the consumer, the cross-border e-commerce firm, and the local partner of that firm.

## CREATING A PREDICTABLE TARIFF AND DELIVERY SYSTEM

South Asia's regulations are not conducive to promoting trade. It has the highest average tariff rates among regions, high tariff dispersion, and nontransparent tariffs, and many countries' trade regimes discriminate against South Asian neighbors. Because intraregional trade is low, the question being asked is whether e-commerce can help to nudge countries to trade more, capitalizing on their shared culture, tastes, proximity, and growing middle class.

A clear de minimis tariff system, preferably with the same threshold across South Asian countries, will help. This would imply zero duties for imports that are valued, say, below US$100. Between the de minimis and a threshold value, the customs clearance process should be simple and clear. For example, all goods valued between US$100 and US$500 could be assessed a simple duty of 10 percent (all figures are illustrative only), with fast-track customs clearance, on the basis of ex ante information exchanged between customs officials and e-commerce firms. These simplified regulations would also help to reduce the congestion at customs arising from growing cross-border parcel shipments.

Given foreign exchange restrictions in several countries, total imports under the de minimis and threshold limits could be subject to a yearly cap per consumer in some countries. Of this cap, perhaps 50 percent could again be reserved for purchases from within South Asia. The cap need not be uniform across countries. The cap could be enforced by e-commerce firms rather than authorities, which would ease the impact on consumers.

Keeping focus on the B2C segment, reduced frictions in delivery of small or parcel shipments will need to accompany simplified tariff regulations. One issue is the high costs of cross-border parcel deliveries (e-commerce-related logistics are a major constraint for cross-border e-commerce sales). Increasing competition and transparency in cross-border parcel services in South Asia, as proposed in the European Union's Digital Single Market strategy, will need to be part of the solution. Moreover, it may be helpful to consult the region's logistics providers on an ongoing basis, extending the European Commission's idea, to develop solutions specific to South Asia. As in the European Union, a regional agreement between South Asian postal service providers could be explored, in due time.

In sum, the final consumer price of products traded via cross-border e-commerce in South Asia can be reduced by easing the tariff framework and making it more predictable, increasing competition in cross-border logistics services, and listening to and incorporating practical suggestions from logistics providers. In addition, in some cases, airports in neighboring countries could be more efficient for cross-border delivery (for example, Varanasi for parts of Nepal), which will require cross-border vehicular access.

## DEVELOPING A REGIONAL MARKET FOR E-TRANSPORT SERVICES

Transport (and logistics) services are not only an input into e-commerce; they also are transacted digitally (e-transport). These services can be made more efficient by allowing cross-border competition and eliminating the restrictions on such trade in South Asia today. Allowing trucks to cross land borders, instead of transloading their cargo, would significantly improve the delivery of parcels. Operationalizing the Bangladesh, Bhutan, India, Nepal Motor Vehicles Agreement (BBIN MVA) would be a good starting point for this process, supplemented by off-border clearances to reduce congestion in land ports. In addition, small and medium-size enterprises (SMEs) can benefit if multiconsignment goods are allowed to be carried in the same truck and off-border clearance of low-value small shipments is permitted.

Another set of reforms could potentially be even more impactful. These would require national regulations, which are currently quite restrictive, to allow hybrid models of goods and passenger transport. Combined with the technological power of app-based aggregator models, this could unleash major efficiency gains (including reduction in costs, congestion, and pollution) through, for example, carrying small shipments in the trunk of a passenger vehicle. In time, this model can be extended to cross-border cooperation in the BBIN region because BBIN MVA applies to goods and passenger services.

## NOTES

1. In some cases, companies may choose the localization model, incorporating in each country. For example, Daraz has local e-commerce entities in Bangladesh, Pakistan, and Sri Lanka. This means that it has decided that each website could offer a different range of products, and that there are currently too many uncertainties in trying to operate in the cross-border space in South Asia.
2. Examples of PISPs include PayPal.

# Final Thoughts

## ENABLING THE (FORMAL) SOUTH ASIA E-COMMERCE MARKET

Informal e-commerce, which mediates tariff and logistics challenges, already takes place within some South Asian countries. This holds promise for the development in South Asia of formal e-commerce, which, unlike informal e-commerce, protects the consumer and can supplement government revenue.

This report has outlined practical steps to kick-start the formal market, as well as more ambitious ideas that could be implemented once the market has taken off. The practical approach involves a combination of the following steps:

- Catalyze the growth of the formal market by permitting cross-border e-commerce payments, perhaps up to a maximum value per consumer and 50 percent reserved for intraregional purchases.
- Institute a de minimis tariff system and a low-value threshold option that is smooth and predictable.
- Pursue flexible transport solutions that allow technology and apps to create efficiency gains and trucks and passenger vehicles to cross land borders.
- Leverage the reputation of large e-commerce platforms to offer consumer protection, return and redress, and data security as an initial substitute for robust contractual and consumer protection mechanisms.
- Start with an incremental approach if necessary—for example, designate an "authorized operator" in e-commerce, with countries mutually agreeing on a list of internationally recognized and nationally reputed companies to get the ball rolling. This approach can help governments and consumers build confidence.

As a cautionary note, an aggressive e-commerce-development strategy can raise some important issues relating to competition. This is especially true in the context of South Asia, where manufacturing capabilities are still at a nascent stage. Clearly, the strengthening of e-commerce in the region will produce significant immediate benefits for consumers, in terms of convenience, variety, and prices. However, the e-commerce space lends itself to substantial economies of both scale and scope, and as such tends to be dominated by a small number of large platforms competing for market share and consumers' data. As of now, the big players in the South Asian market are competing fiercely to boost sales and build customer loyalty, which in practice translates into offers of ever-better deals, the provision of "free" ancillary services, and the adoption of consumer-friendly business practices. Quite predictably, however, most or all of these firms are currently not making profits, as the medium-term strategy is for them to burn money now to eventually become market leaders later. How long it will take until this happens, and what consequences will derive from this reorganization of the market structure is, however, a subject for debate. Therefore, a strategy for South Asian integration should feature a review of competition policy in the region, to account for the quasi-natural monopoly nature of the e-commerce market.

Relatedly, like every trade openness measure, e-commerce is also exposing the South Asian domestic economies to import competition from abroad. Despite the usual portrait of e-commerce as a booster of domestic production and as a tool for the integration of small and medium entrepreneurs into larger markets, there are questions surrounding this in the South Asian landscape. In particular, consultations with e-commerce platforms in the region revealed that most of the merchandise being sold online comes from third countries (especially from China) rather than being produced by local manufacturers. Although this may represent just an organic development as opening to trade rearranges the specialization patterns of the countries involved, it is also possible that these dynamics may stifle domestic production more than proportionally. Extra care should be taken, therefore, to ensure that the interests of small, national producers are not unduly sacrificed for the sake of short-term consumer gains. A promising strategy in this respect would be to invest in the development of e-commerce-intensive productive sectors in which South Asia enjoys a comparative advantage in the eyes of South Asian consumers. These could be products that bundle goods with strong services (for example, design, or after-sales services), content goods (like entertainment products), or those products that are less standardized and customized to local tastes. The question then remains whether e-commerce could nurture these products, enabling them to flourish both in exports and in the import-competing space.